Life Abundant

Life Abundant

PAUL R. DEKAR

RESOURCE *Publications* • Eugene, Oregon

LIFE ABUNDANT

Copyright © 2025 Paul R. Dekar. All rights reserved. Except for brief quotations in critical publications or reviews, no part of this book may be reproduced in any manner without prior written permission from the publisher. Write: Permissions, Wipf and Stock Publishers, 199 W. 8th Ave., Suite 3, Eugene, OR 97401.

Resource Publications
An Imprint of Wipf and Stock Publishers
199 W. 8th Ave., Suite 3
Eugene, OR 97401

www.wipfandstock.com

PAPERBACK ISBN: 979-8-3852-2098-4
HARDCOVER ISBN: 979-8-3852-2099-1
EBOOK ISBN: 979-8-3852-2100-4

02/18/26

I dedicate this book to Nancy Rose Dekar, my best friend and life partner. Nancy often cites medieval German theologian Meister Eckhart, "If the only prayer you said was thank you, that would be enough." With this in mind, Nancy, thank you for your compassion, humility, and love.

Contents

	Abbreviations	ix
	Timeline	xi
	Introduction	1
1	Father	5
2	Mother	11
3	Sister	18
4	Brother	22
5	Nancy Jean Rose	25
6	Nathaniel and Family	33
7	Matthew and Family	37
8	Russian Orthodox Religious Roots	40
9	Jewish Religious Roots	43
10	The Arts	49
11	My Friend Russ	52
12	Early Education	54
13	University of California, Berkeley	59
14	Free Speech Movement	66
15	1962 APBA Season	69
16	Yellowstone National Park, 1962 and 2023	72
17	Camp Counselor	75
18	Organizing for Change	77
19	Operation Crossroads Africa, Chad	81
20	Seminary	85

Contents

21	Flower City Conspiracy	90
22	Foreign Service Officer	92
23	Ministry and Ordination	96
24	Graduate School	98
25	Teaching and Sabbaticals	101
26	Religious Communities	111
27	Servant Leadership	116
28	Monastic Journey	119
29	Two Lakes	123
30	Community Activities	127
31	Gandhian *Swadeshi* in Colombia	132
32	Tomato Soup and Grilled Cheese Sandwiches	137
33	Reflections on Turning Eighty	139
34	Dream of God and Concluding Reflections	142

Appendix 1: Las Lomas graduation address, 1961, Ever the Faith Endures — 147

Appendix 2: Application for Conscientious Objector Status, June 1, 1967 — 149

Appendix 3: Ordination Paper, excerpted, May 5, 1971 — 151

Appendix 4: "My Journey in Peacemaking," *Waging Peace in Hamilton*, 2017 — 155

Archival Sources and Bibliography — 161

Abbreviations

AGO	Alpha Gamma Omega
ABC	American Baptist Churches
A. F. S.	American Field Service
BPFNA	Baptist Peace Fellowship of North America
CCC	Canadian Council of Churches
CFSC	Canadian Friends Service Committee
CMU	Central Michigan University
CIRG	Christian Interfaith Reference Group
c. o.	conscientious objector
CRDS	Colgate Rochester Divinity School
D. C.	District of Colombia
DPI	Democracy Probe International
FOR	Fellowship of Reconciliation
FSO	foreign service officer
FSM	Free Speech Movement
J. S. A.	Junior Statesmen of America
KRA	Kirkendall Recreation Association
MAD	mutually assured destruction
MDC	McMaster Divinity College
MTS	Memphis Theological Seminary

Abbreviations

OCA	Operation Crossroads Africa
USSR	Union of Soviet Socialist Republics
US	United States of America
UCB	University of California, Berkeley
UCD	University of California, Davis

Timeline

October 31, 1892	birth maternal grandfather Spiradon [Spira] Dovjenko in Ukraine
July 5, 1895	birth paternal grandmother Vera Perelonoff Dovjenko in Russia
July 14, 1896	birth step-grandfather Trofim [Tommy] Kroviakoff in Russia
January 1, 1898	birth maternal grandmother Margaret Arkadivna Burstein in Russia
May 5, 1916	birth father, Paul Georgievich [Gregory] Dekarhonoff in Chita, Siberia
July 19, 1916	birth mother, Ariadne [Ada] Dovjenko Dekar in Kiev, Ukraine
February 8, 1944	my birth in San Francisco, California
February 2, 1946	birth wife Nancy Jean Rose Dekar in Barton, New York
November 9, 1946	birth sister, Marguerite Jean Dekar Li in San Francisco
September 16, 1948	birth brother, George Steven Dekar in San Francisco
1952	family move from San Francisco to Walnut Creek, Contra Costa County
1957–1961	attended Las Lomas High School

Timeline

1961–1965	attended University of California, Berkeley; awarded B. A. with a major in Political Science
1965–67, 1970–71	attended Colgate Rochester Divinity School; awarded M. Div.
1968–1970	United States Department of State posting in Cameroon
September 23, 1970	death father
April 1, 1971	ordination, Monroe Baptist Association of Rochester, New York
December 27, 1971	birth son Nathaniel Paul Dekar, Chicago, Illinois
1971–1975	attended University of Chicago; awarded M. A, 1973 and Ph. D., 1978
1975–1976	taught Central Michigan University, Mt. Pleasant, Michigan
1975	death grandfather Tommy Kroviakoff
February 25, 1977	death grandfather Spira Dovjenko
February 27, 1977	death grandmother Vera Dovjenko
1976–1994	taught, McMaster Divinity College and McMaster University, Hamilton, Ontario, Canada; named Centenary Professor of World Christianity
April 16, 1979	birth son Matthew Paul Dekar, Hamilton, Ontario
1991–1992	Acting Director, Centre for Peace Studies, McMaster University
June 23, 1993	death grandmother Margaret Kroviakoff
1995–2008	taught, Memphis Theological Seminary, Memphis, Tennessee; named Niswonger Professor of Evangelism and Mission

Timeline

1999–2008	adjunct professor, University of Memphis
November 16, 1999	death mother
December 19, 1999	Nathaniel and Jackie Dekar wedding
May 23, 2001	birth granddaughter Abigail Jack-Ellen Dekar
June 18, 2003	birth granddaughter Emma Jessamine Dekar
2008	retired; named emeritus professor; returned to Hamilton, Ontario, Canada
August 25, 2012	wedding Matthew and Melissa Dekar
August 20, 2014	birth grandson Drake Matthew Dekar
July 4, 2016	birth granddaughter Nadine Camille Dekar

Introduction

IN *THE LITTLE PRINCE* by Antoine de Saint-Exupéry a fox shares "a very simple secret. It is only with the heart that one can see rightly; what is essential is invisible to the eye." The little prince repeats, "What is essential is invisible to the eye." The fox continues, "Men have forgotten this truth. . . . But you must not forget it. You become responsible, forever, for what you have tamed. You are responsible for your rose."[1]

As individuals and members of larger groups and nation states, we have failed our responsibility to care for our rose, our fragile planet. As I write, catastrophic climate change, wars, the possession of nuclear weapons by a growing number of countries, economic uncertainty, human rights violations, notably in the US and Canada with respect to indigenous peoples, and threats to democracy are deeply worrisome. We can and must do much better to care for our precious but precarious home.

As a theme for this memoir, I have chosen Jesus' words "life abundant." Responding to controversy over his identity and ministry, the Gospel of John recorded Jesus as saying, "The thief comes only to steal and kill and destroy. I came that they may have life, and have it abundantly" (John 10:10). Similarly, the apostle Paul wrote to the church at Corinth, "And God is able to provide you with every blessing in abundance, so that by always having enough of everything, you may share abundantly in every good work" (2 Cor 9:8).

The life abundant leitmotif is central as well in Hebrew Scripture. Deuteronomy 30:19–20 records Moses summoning the

---

1. Saint-Exupéry, *Little Prince*, 70–71.

Israelites as follows, "I call heaven and earth to witness against you this day, that I have set before you life and death, blessing and curse; therefore choose life, that you and your descendants may live."

In *Psalms for a Pilgrim People*, Anglican priest Jim Cotter encapsulates the theme in his rendering of Psalm 67 as follows, "O God of wise judgment, accepting us as we are and guiding us in your ways, enable us so to appreciate your gifts . . . that we may know them as a pledge of abundant life and thank you as the source and goal of all that is good."[2] I trust that readers may resonate with this key Biblical theme and respond positively to my concern that the rights, peace, and security of all persons be respected.

I am sharing from my personal history stories that identify people and experiences foundational to my lifelong commitment to human rights, peace and the integrity of creation. My family background is Russian. The revolution of 1917, a major event that still affects the world, had an enormous impact on ancestors like mine who lived in Russia and had to deal with the turmoil directly. Lives were changed and many families were permanently split up. Remnants of my family fled to Yugoslavia, Manchuria in northeast China, North and South America. The fate of many family members is unknown and probably unrecoverable.

During the Fall of 1958, I attended a Billy Graham crusade at the Cow Palace in San Francico. I was fourteen years old and a sophomore in high school. As the gathering ended, I left but felt moved to return. When I went forward, Counsellor Paul Lindholm met and prayed with me. Subsequently, he visited my home several times for *Bible* study. I subscribed to *Decision*, a publication of the Billy Graham Evangelistic Association. I joined a Baptist church to which I could walk or bike.

In 1995, when I was teaching at McMaster University in Hamilton, Ontario, I joined a group that invited Dr. Graham to the area. During his visit, I had a chance to talk privately with him. I acknowledged his importance in my spiritual journey. I added that, having attended a university and seminary deemed liberal in some circles, I had moved theologically from the more

---

2. Cotter, *Psalms*, 139.

Introduction

conservative stance associated with him. Dr. Graham assured me this was natural. We prayed together. As we parted, Dr. Graham blessed me and said that, from what I had shared, mine was truly life abundant.

In early chapters of this memoir, I introduce my parents, their coming to North America and how they adapted to a new world. I am grateful that neither Dad, nor Mom, nor any other relative expressed anger or desire to avenge circumstances that had led them to flee Russia.

After brief stories about my upbringing, marriage, and family, other chapters explore aspects of my life pertinent to the theme. Most vignettes are original, with four exceptions. Chapter 27 has material from *Holy Boldness, Practices of an Evangelistic Lifestyle* (Macon, 2004). Chapter 31 appeared in McMaster University's Seventeenth Gandhi Peace Festival brochure. As I have been part of several delegation to conflict zones, I chose to highlight my journey to Colombia where our mission was to offer protective accompaniment to members of a community that was, and remains vulnerable. Chapter 34 appeared in *Journeying with Hope into a New Year: Reflections for Advent and Christmas* (Eugene, 2022). Anne M. Pearson, Khursheed Ahmed and Joy Warner included Appendix 4, "My Journey in Peacemaking" in *Waging Peace in Hamilton* (Hamilton, 2017).

As sources, I have drawn on correspondence, transcriptions of interviews, notebooks, and personal diaries that I have maintained since 1979 when I participated in an intensive journal workshop led by Ira Progoff. I am grateful for the encouragement and editorial advice given my sister Marguerite Jean Li and her husband Stacy. Friends Darlene James and Ron Morissey provided additional editorial help. One-time students and long-time friends LeeAnn McKenna and Barry Morrison contributed words for this book's dust jacket. I am responsible for the final manuscript. When quoting other sources, I do not alter non-inclusive texts. For scripture, I cite the *New Revised Standard Bible*.

1

Father

MY FATHER, PAUL GEORGIEVICH (Gregory) Dekarhonoff (May 5, 1916-September 23, 1970), was born in Chita, Siberia of Armenian and Russian ancestry. His father Gregory Dekarhonoff Lenkovsky worked on the Trans-Siberian Railroad.[1] Due to the harsh Siberian winter, Dad's mother Maria often put him in a home-made cradle over a wood-burning stove. This was an unsafe practice with the result that, as an infant, Dad rolled into a pot of boiling water. A toe had to be amputated. Later, this proved serendipitous. While Dad did not manifest evidence of disability, he was disqualified to serve in the military during the Second World War.

Sometime after 1917, when the "Reds" took control of the country, Gregory and Maria were civilian casualties of the Russian Revolution.[2] Possibly they were regarded as "Whites," when the

---

1. *Dersu Uzala* won the 1975 Oscar in the best foreign language film category. An international production, it drew on a memoir by a Mongolian hunter who shepherded the team building the Trans-Siberian Railroad across the Caucasus Mountains and thus portrayed conditions Dad and his family might have experienced.

2. Another film, *Reds* (1981), based on a book by John Reed, *Ten Days That Shook the World*, tells the story of a journalist active in the Communist Party who died in a Russian hospital of tuberculosis and kidney failure. The book and film provide a narrative of the November 2017 revolution in Russia, emphasizing the seizure of power by the Communists and subsequent social upheaval.

"Reds" killed Nicholas II, the last Russian emperor along with his wife, Alexandra, and their children.

Before Maria died, she handed my father to a relative, Vera Pavlovna Dekarhanova (1895–1977), and asked her to raise Paul as her own son. In effect, though not in law, father's aunt Vera and her first husband Paul Zachary Dekarhanoff adopted him. Vera later married my Mother's father, Spiradon Dovjenko.

Around 1922, Dad's family was able to flee Siberia with his relatives Vera and Paul Dekarhanoff, a relative of Vera, Luba Siberiakoff, who I knew as Aunt Luba, and Genadie W. Stepanoff, who became my God-father. In 1975, Grandmother Vera wrote a letter in which she explained the circumstances, as follows,

> Dear Ricky,[3] lest I forget, I like to tell you some more about your family. . . . Parents of your father were Maria and Gregory Dekarhanoff Lenkovsky, who died when your father was a child. We met before my marriage to Spira. Gregory sent us money to come to America. He was a dancer. We fled from Siberia, we *run* [her emphasis] from revolution to Shanghai, living on money Paul's father borrows (took) from his regiment. He had been trusted with money to deliver to another town. We ran from the south of Russia, where he was fighting Reds on Whites' side—that was before we run to Shanghai and then to the US. Some time, I tell you more about all of Dekarhonoffs; you can write a book about them. It was so much happening.

In a similar letter to my sister, Vera explained that that they had to dress like ordinary people, thus deflecting attention from their elite status in Tsarist Russia. Continuing, Vera wrote:

> All Russia was on the move, people frightened, bewildered. All trains in constant move, army moving from town to town. So you just got the train with ticket or not, and move nearer to Siberia and China if lucky–or

---

3. Father and I shared the same first name. Growing up, I was often called by my middle name, Richard, Ricky or Rick. In naming our sons, Nancy and I incorporated my first name into theirs, hence Nathaniel Paul Dekar and Matthew Paul Dekar.

be killed. Travel have been free in old Russia too. Now no freedom in Russia.

The party likely traveled on the Chinese Eastern Railway linking Chita with Harbin, Manchuria, and found their way to Yokohama, Japan. In 1922, they sailed to the US and settled in San Francisco, California. Upon arrival in North America, Dad's uncle Paul abandoned the family. On March 11, 1932, Grandmother Vera married Spiridon Gregorovich Dovjenko. In an obituary published in a San Francisco paper, Vera called Dad her son.

In the years when he was growing up, Dad attended Lick Wilmerding High School. By then, his name had been shortened to Paul Dekar. For a while, he sold newspapers. During harvest season, he worked in the Salinas Valley south of San Francisco, an area known for the quality of vegetables like asparagus, lettuce, and garlic.

In the early 1940s, Dad met Ariadne (Ada) Dovjenko, who had come to San Francisco to visit her biological father and stepmother, Spira and Vera Dovjenko. A courtship followed and, February 28, 1943, the couple married. On February 8, 1944, I was the firstborn of three siblings. Marguerite Jean (born November 9, 1946) and our late brother George Steven (September 16, 1948-February 18, 2003) followed.

Ariadne's mother Margaret did not approve of her daughter's choice of a husband. Controlling and manipulative, Margaret criticized Dad at every opportunity and clearly believed that he was not good enough, smart enough, or of sufficiently high social standing to be Ariadne's life partner.

Our family vacations often involved a visit to Seattle with Ariadne's mother Margaret and stepfather Tom Kroviakoff. Disagreements erupted, after which we would abruptly return to California. These arguments caused unnecessary strains on family life and took their toll on everyone. Dad sometimes left the house for a few days. Each time he returned, but I always feared he might not. In the end, I understood that Dad loved mother and our family so much that he could not abandon us.

Dad learned lithography, now a fine art, and partnered with Phil Rude. Their shop was located in the Market area of San Francisco. Dad designed menus for restaurant owners. When our family dined at establishments for which Dad had a professional relationship, clients greeted us and sometimes paid for our meal. After Rude's death by suicide, Dad kept the shop and took pride in being able to provide income for our family. There was always enough to meet our basic needs.

Around 1952, we moved from San Francisco to Walnut Creek in Contra Costa County, at the time a rural area dotted with creeks, hills, and walnut groves. Living about sixteen miles (some twenty-six kilometers) east of Oakland, Dad car pooled to work in a black Cadillac. We were located the furthest from San Francisco, so the Caddie was parked at our house. Dad drove the car, picked up the other commuters, and was the last to get home. We knew when he returned due to the tire noise on our gravel driveway.

Dad developed many hobbies. A brilliant photographer, Dad regularly exhibited his prints. In 1947, San Francisco's M. H. de Young Museum featured one of his best, "The Morning Ride." The next year, Dad served as President of the California Camera Club and as an instructor in an annual eight-week course. In 1949, he received a statue for third-place in the club's monthly competition.

Dad wrote a regular column, "Prexy's Message" in the club's newsletter, *The View Finder*. He advised how to improve nature or portrait photographs. In "Paul Dekar: Photographer and Teacher," an article published in the *San Francisco Chronicle* on February 27, 1949, Dad stated that he was often up early to take advantage of natural light. The article featured "Architecture and Texture" that he had photographed in Victoria, British Colombia, Canada.

Dad taught me to develop black-and-white prints. I was saddened when, after his death, Mom sold or gave away Dad's gear that I had hoped one day to use. I cannot speculate how Dad would have felt about adapting to digital photography.

My father was also a swimmer. Every New Years' Day when still living in San Francisco, he jumped into the frigid Pacific Ocean waters to welcome the passing of another year.

Another pastime was music. Dad listened to operas and operettas on long-playing albums or on the radio. His favorite musicians were Italian tenor Enrico Caruso and American tenor Mario Lanza. As well, he took us to a variety of concerts including opera and orchestra. Each summer after our move to Walnut Creek, we attended open-air concerts in the foothills overlooking Oakland.

I still play an album of Mario Lanza's *Christmas Hymns* and other of Dad's vinyl in our music library. Dad especially enjoyed Handel's *Messiah*. First performed around Easter, many listen during Advent. My sister Peg once saw me in my room doing homework and listening to the *Messiah* on a small radio nearby. She recalled this story, "I love this memory."

Dad took our family to movies. In addition, Mom and Dad enjoyed casual gambling at casinos along the Nevada shore of Lake Tahoe, or in Reno, Nevada. Peg, George, and I watched kid-friendly cinema, provided as "baby-sitting." While I enjoyed most films, some had images of dangerous critters, car chases, or explosions. These sparked nightmares well into adulthood.

Dad loved chess and taught me to play. In one of my last times with him, after the second of his two heart attacks, we played chess in his hospital room. Dad won, as he always did! For many years I continued to play and taught my older granddaughters Abbey and Emma, who played chess at school.

Dad organized outings to the Sierra Nevada mountain range and, closer to home, to Big Sur State Park and Big Basin Redwoods State Park south of San Francisco or Muir Woods State Park north of the city. We loved camping under towering redwoods, alders, cottonwood, maple, oaks, sycamore, and willow trees. Such enjoyment of the outdoors has pervaded our family. Sons Nathaniel and Matthew, my sister, and their families similarly love the outdoors.

Dad was scout master for my Cub and Boy Scout packs. We enjoyed our hikes, and Dad helped me earn several merit badges. He never expressed disappointment that I did not become an Eagle Scout. He understood my priorities then were study, campus politics, sports, driving, and dating.

Life Abundant

Dad once served on a jury that convicted someone who was ultimately executed. Dad came to regard the death penalty as a violation of human rights. That position influenced my thinking on this, as well as on other issues.

In the mid 1960s, Dad and Mom moved from Walnut Creek to Rheem Valley, which was later incorporated into the town of Moraga. At the time, I lived away from home as a university student and so was unaware why my parents moved. My mother was a real estate agent as well as lab technician at Kaiser Hospital so she likely recognized the relative low price of the homes in this new real estate development. Also, the town was in the news because a modern cinema theater had been built there. That may have brought the area to Mom and Dad's attention. They may have simply wanted a change or were planning ahead for the time when they would be empty nesters. One benefit was a shorter distance Dad had to travel to and from work.

Before attending my marriage to Nancy on New Years Eve, December 31, 1967, Dad and Mom visited Washington, D. C. They toured important sites in the nation's capital where I lived a few months after my appointment as foreign service officer with the US State Department.

My first posting was in Cameroon, Africa. The distance separated me from family for over two and a half years. After Nancy and I returned from Cameroon to North America, I managed to see Dad several times in hospital before he died from his second and ultimately fatal heart attack. He was only fifty-four years old.

Every one who met Dad, even briefly, called him a good man. I always felt close to him and have never ceased to grieve his death at so early an age, nor to lament our not having been able to form a relationship in my adult years. Dad would have enjoyed being part of my family with Nancy, our sons and their families.

Framed copies of several of Dad's black and white photos grace our home. Despite having lived away from home since I left for university, I have continued to draw strength from Dad's love and life-giving humanitarianism. Dad thus continues to be a pillar of my life abundant. *Deo gratias!*

2

Mother

MY MOTHER, ARIADNE [ADA] Dovjenko Dekar (July 19, 1916-November 16, 1999), was born in Kiev, Ukraine which was then part of the Russian empire. Her parents were Spiradon (Spira) Grigorovich Dovjenko (1892-1977), a Russian Orthodox Christian born in Berislav, Ukraine near the mouth of the Dnieper River, and Margaret Burstein Dovjenko, or Marusia (1898-1995), a Jew born in Nizhneudinsk, Siberia.

Spira trained as an engineer at a technical school in the city of Nikolaev. He may have attended a military academy in Odessa. During World War I, he served in the Russian army as an officer and civil engineer. He designed bridges. Around November 15, 1915, he married Margaret Burstein. For several years, Spira and Margaret lived in Kiev where their daughter, my mother Ariadne was born.

Margaret was the daughter of Gregory Burstein and Eve Kushner. The oldest of four children, she was a brilliant student and received a gold medal in secondary school. As "White Russians" who maintained their loyalty to the Tsar, she and her family were unsafe during the Bolshevik Revolution. So Spira, Margaret, and Mom fled, first to Siberia through which they traveled east on the Trans-Siberian Railroad.

I can only imagine the terror that prevailed as they arrived at the station. Confusion reigned. Soldiers and families rushed to board the train to head east. "Hurry, Marusia, we must go. The train will be here soon. Leave that, it is too heavy to carry." "But Spira, I'm not ready. Please hold Adochka. Aunt Leah isn't here. I want to say good-bye to my sister. I don't know when I'll see her again."

Facing days of travel, Spira assured Margaret that everything would be ok. Sometimes they traveled together, and sometimes apart. Eventually, they crossed the border south of Chita, Siberia and headed to Harbin, Manchuria, where Spira worked on locomotives. They stayed there a few years until they were able to earn sufficient funds for travel and to attain visas to enter the US.

The family departed from Yokohama, Japan on the S. S. President Jackson and docked in Seattle, Washington on September 1, 1923. They were among six thousand refugees who arrived from Russia in Seattle that year. US government quotas at the time prevented them from sponsoring other family members to join them in North America. It was more than thirty years before my mother reunited with a few relatives.

Trofim (Tommy) Gavrilovich Kroviakoff (1892–1975) was another passenger during the crossing to the US. Trofim was an officer in the Imperial Russian Army and served on the German front from 1915 until 1917. During the Russian civil war, he served in the White Army.

Tommy and Spira knew each other in Harbin. Crossing the Pacific, Mom's mother switched partners. Once settled in the US, Margaret filed for divorce in order to marry Tommy. After his marriage ended July 22, 1925, Spira quit work at the Washington Iron Works, left Seattle, and moved to San Francisco to begin a new life. According to my sister, "I had the impression that Margaret was more than a flirt. However, she may simply have had her eye out for anyone. I never knew why Spira dissatisfied her. War, then revolution, quite a mix. No wonder life was disrupted."

Margaret's brother David Burstein, his wife Olga, and their daughter Eva remained in China until the Chinese Communist Party ascended to power in 1949 after several decades of war. In a letter dated May 3, 1993, Eva provided a snapshot of Mother's early years.

Mother

Dearest Adachka, I have many stories from my father who enjoyed sharing them with me. I can relate that time when your parents left you with our babushka [grandmother] Eva. You were but an infant. You remained with my father, grandmother, and aunts Katia and Leah. At that time aunt Leah was heading to Tomsk to study pediatric medicine and married Vladimir Samkin. They had the two daughters, Inna and Irene, the latter perishing in the Holocaust with our Aunt Leah when they separated from Inna and Vladimir to volunteer her services in Brest Litovsk. I have written the German government to please locate where and when their deaths took place.

Pappa did spend a lot of time reading and teaching you things. You were a delightful child bringing much joy to our grandmother, your uncle, and aunts. Pappa said that you were very bright and inquisitive. You adored Pappa and when he was studying you used to like to climb on his lap and scribble in his books and notebooks. In fact he used to tell me that a few times without him being aware of it. When he would discover you drawing and reprimand you, you would call out to our grandmother saying "Davidchik is not permitting me to draw in his "jivoyo slovo" [Russian for word book.]

I thought you might like to hear some of these beautiful events that transpired in your childhood. You too were there for Pappa's small but important land mark, his Bar Mitzvah, poor as they were living from hand to hand without a father. You know our grandfather Grisha [Gregory] was ninety-six years old when Pappa was only six. What a virile grandpa we had! He was a furrier and also worked in a kosher slaughter house. Beautiful memories from the many stories Pappa shared. I miss him beyond description. I still get letters, cards, and donations. He was loved by all. Hugs, Eva

Upon arrival in Seattle, Washington, Mom adapted well to her new country, which offered freedom and opportunity. Mom's stepfather worked for the Boeing Company, which was then, and has remained among the largest aerospace manufacturers worldwide. Margaret worked as a laundress. Despite having learned English only in her teens, Mom was precocious. She skipped a grade in high school and graduated from the University of Washington in 1936 at the young age of twenty with a degree in microbiology. For a few years, she worked as a lab technician in Seattle.

Around 1942, Mom visited her biological father Spira who had moved to San Francisco where he had married Vera Pavlovna Dekar. Spira worked in real estate and, simultaneously, as an insurance agent. It is claimed that he was the one who first one to install neon lights on Juke boxes that formerly looked just like ordinary furniture.

Spira's investments in San Francisco's Haight-Ashbury and Sunset districts did well. He bought property and then traded up for better properties. In 1960 he bought his last property, an apartment building on 38th Avenue in the Richmond district. Another focus of his life was to locate the scattered relatives and sponsor them for immigration to the US. Grandmother Vera worked in a millinery factory.

When mother visited her father, Vera asked her nephew Paul to help host Ariadne. Sparks flew and a brief courtship followed. Mom and Dad married February 27, 1943. A year later, on February 8, 1944, I was the firstborn of three children.

As I grew up, Mom's primary role was that of a housewife. Cooking and baking were a central part of her life and provided us a sense of abundance in our lives. Mom loved to organize and prepare for parties. Even during times of illness and convalescence after surgery, she provided hearty meals for herself, Dad and George after Peg and I moved on to university.

Mom's pirozhki and pierogi, divinity and fudge, pralines and apricot-almond bars, jams and cakes were something special. At Easter, Mom prepared kulich (a sweet bread) and paskha (a cheese cake). Nancy has continued to make the latter in a wooden frame that I made for Grandmother Vera seventy years ago.

Mom's role expanded after Phil Rude, Dad's business partner, committed suicide and the business struggled. Our family income was reduced, but there was a house mortgage to cover. By that time, we lived in Walnut Creek. As a result, Mom worked part-time from noon until six as a lab technician with Kaiser Permanente Hospital, which was located a short walk from Las Lomas High School where my sister Peg and I attended secondary school, or Parkmead where our George was in primary school. Before going to work, Mom prepared the dinners and sometimes treats in coordination with Peg. Then Peg warmed the food in time for the family supper. After dinner, Mom would prepare the next day's meals and sometimes bake bread or cookies.

Then George was diagnosed with schizophrenia. George's illness was so severe that he eventually was incapable of living or working independently. Mom brought him home and cared for him for about thirty years. This was demanding. George would frequently leave home and wander. Mom would not know where he was, how long he was going to be away, or whether he would return. This tested all her strength and was a measure of her capacity to love.

My mother's relationship with her mother was unhealthy. Mom was always seeking approval that never came. This dynamic was incorporated into Mom's emotional structure, so she seemed to mimic her mother at times and never freed herself entirely from Margaret's influence. Arguments with her mother weakened Mom emotionally, caused unnecessary turmoil between Mom and Dad, and engendered strains in her relationships with all her children. She found it difficult to recognize or celebrate our achievements or even to listen to us. Often when I tried to share something, I was told to shut up.

Mother struggled with her own health issues, especially asthma. It took me a long time to come to terms with mother's wild swings of mood. At one point, I undertook counseling. I came to understand the extent Mom had been abused by her mother and to see Mom as a loving and caring person for whom duty and responsibility were important.

Enjoying travel, Mom especially appreciated the beauty of Oregon, where she and Dad bought land along the Rogue River. Before Dad's death, they talked of retirement there. After Dad died, Mom sold the property. She briefly tried her hand in real estate while continuing her career as a microbiologist.

Life Abundant

In retirement, Mother read prodigiously. Active with Moraga Hacienda Seniors, Mom wrote book reviews for its newsletter and joined trips to Michigan, Mount Rushmore, eastern Washington state, British Colombia, New Orleans, Louisiana, and Memphis, Tennessee where she took delight visiting Graceland and eating at a steakhouse frequented by Elvis Presley. Two weeks before she died, she traveled to Reno, where she won a little at the five-cent slots and penny poker.

While not active politically, Mom always voted. Around 1970, she wrote "an open letter to my fellow citizens" that reflected her liberal bent and loyalty to the US. She emphatically questioned the war in Vietnam. "I know the bitterness that follows wars . . . fellow Americans, where do we go from here?"

Mom volunteered with the Mt. Diablo Peace Center. She supported causes like Christian Children's Fund through which she sponsored a Guatemalan girl Lydia Judith Gonzales. Her generosity and support for liberal causes grew from her innate compassion and spirituality.

Mom was generous to family, friend, or anyone in need. She never failed to provide gifts for birthdays and holidays. As my sister and I lived at a distance with our families, Mom diligently sent parcels and funds. She abounded in witticisms and doggerel that she shared with a joking, easy tone of voice and an infectious laugh. I still can remember her smiling as she said,

> I eat my peas with honey,
> I've done it all my life.
> It makes them taste funny
> But it keeps them on the knife.

In the Fall of 1999, while I was teaching a class in Memphis, I learned that Mom was near death. I hastened to her hospital bedside. Mother squeezed my hand and sought assurance that I would look after my brother George, for whom she had cared for years after his diagnosis of schizophrenia. I promised that I would. A month later during the marriage of her grandson Nathaniel to Jackie Miller, we lit a candle in her memory.

Mother

At a celebration of her life, Larry Michaelson, a member of Valley Baptist Church in Walnut Creek, attested to abundance in her life. Larry recalled that mother worked at the same hospital with his wife Laverne. "They saw each other often. Ariadne was always jolly at work." Larry said that Ariadne generally came to church early, which gave them a chance to chat. "Ariadne minced no words. You knew where she stood. In politics you knew what her political party was and it didn't begin with an R." Larry spoke of her pride in her family concluding, "We will miss her and we are thankful for her life."

Mother is buried at the Oakmont Cemetery in Pleasant Hill next to Dad and my brother George and near the columbarium that houses the ashes of her mother Margaret. When able, I visit their grave sites. I offer a prayer of gratitude for Mom and Dad who ensured that I and my siblings received an abundance of love, a thorough education, and a good start in life. *Deo gratias!*

3

Sister

MARGUERITE JEAN (PEG) DEKAR Li was born on November 9, 1946. Growing up, we developed a deep friendship. In several black and white photos of us, Dad captured a sense of abundance and joy. One print, entitled Shadows, hangs in our home. Peg and I were walking hand in hand with elongated shadows trailing behind us. Others in my earliest scrapbook show us together, or with George, enjoying family celebrations and our trips, notably to Lake Tahoe.

Peg graduated in 1964 in the top five of her Las Lomas High School class. She went on to the Davis campus of the University of California (UCD) from which she graduated in 1968 with a major in psychology and a minor in biology.

Peg was born to be a teacher. She taught elementary school at Linda School near in Marysville, California, followed by Rhoda Maxwell School in Woodland, Rock Creek School in Auburn and Alta Vista School in Auburn. While teaching at Alta Vista, she attended night school in Sacramento, the state capital. In 1977, she completed a Master of Arts in Education.

Peg met her future husband, Stacy Li, in a class at UCD. He often said, "The only thing I got out of my botany class was my wife." Stacy worked as an environmental consultant in aquatic biology for four different firms.

When Peg decided to marry Stacy, of Chinese background, she met high resistance from Grandmother Margaret and our Mother. Dad was caught in the middle between his wife and his daughter and could not attend Peg and Stacy's wedding. Mom and Grandmother Margaret moderated their venom only after Peg had children. Grandmother Margaret said of her great grandchildren, "They are of my blood." Mother claimed Stacy was her favorite son-in-law. While Stacy was her favorite by default, he has observed that it was more important that they became friends.

Peg provided essential support for Stacy, who founded Aquatic Systems Research in 1989 for which he consulted and performed research on environmental issues. He served as California Fish and Game's expert witness on instream flow issues in the Mono Lake hearings. Another job was instream flow assessments of the Tuolumne River, a class III white water river.

In 2001, Stacy joined the National Marine Fisheries Service as a fish ecologist and water rights specialist. He sought to conserve and manage fisheries, promote sustainability and prevent lost economic potential associated with overfishing, declining species, or degraded habitats. Stacy retired in 2008.

Peg and Stancy had two children. Born December 12, 1979, Marina Christine Li graduated as class valedictorian in 1998 from Del Oro High School in Loomis, California. She continued her education at Mills College, a private liberal arts and sciences college for women in Oakland, California where she majored in Social Justice and was the outstanding senior when she graduated in 2002. Marina pursued a career in the arts and, at the time of writing, is focused on her family. She has given birth to two children, Dimitri Li-Santos, born April 20, 2012 (father Valfredo Santos) and Kyla Li Rafferty, born August 10, 2016 (father Brian Rafferty).

Born June 29, 1981, Burton David Li attended Del Oro High School. As a junior Burton participated in the American Legion Boys State. Elected Governor by his peers, Burton then went on to Boy's Nation and personally met President Bill Clinton and Senator Barbara Boxer.

Life Abundant

Graduating in 1999, Burton was valedictorian like his sister. He continued his education at the Santa Cruz campus of the University of California and graduated in 2003 with a BA in cultural anthropology. On September 29, 2012, he married Trupti Salukhe. Trupti and Burton have two children, Vera Nova (born August 20, 2014) and Cassian River (born May 22, 2018).

At the time of writing, Burton and Trupti live both in Truckee, California in the Sierra Nevada mountains, and in San Francisco where they manage the apartment building once owned by Grandfather Spira and Grandmother Vera Dovjenko. In addition, Burton is principal of Sutro Li, an accounting business serving nonprofit organizations.

It is a miracle that my sister safely bore two children. Years earlier, she suffered four consecutive first trimester miscarriages. Then she nearly died due to complications of what proved to be a life-threatening ectopic pregnancy during which an embryo was implanted outside the uterine cavity. Her ruptured fallopian tube pregnancy resulted in loss of a great deal of blood that was life threatening.

After Mom died, Peg took on major responsibility for the care of our brother George. She also moved Grandmother Margaret to California, initially to Moraga, then to San Francisco to what had been Grandfather Spira's apartment, then to Loomis and finally to assisted living. Thanksgivings were a challenge. For several years Peg and her family went to Moraga for an early meal, then to San Francisco to have another with Margaret and finally to Stacy's parents for a third feast.

In retirement, Peg and Stacy live in Santa Rosa, California. Peg still applies her teaching skills on her grandchildren. Other major commitments include involvement in a United Methodist congregation and gardening at Harvest for the Hungry, which provides organic produce for those in need. She once explained, "I just jumped in!" Through her support for homeless people on the streets of their city and other such engagements, Peg has lived her Christian faith and exemplified the life abundant in which our parents nurtured us and our spiritual journeys.

Sister

As I conclude this chapter, I want especially to express gratitude for Peg who assumed great responsibilities for Grandmother Margaret, notably in the face of abuse, and for George whose mental illness developed after I had moved away from California. I cannot imagine how much more difficult their situations would have been without Peg's loving care.

As well, over many years, Peg connected with several relatives, notably cousin Natasha Sharkov who lived nearby in San Anselmo, a short drive from Santa Rosa, and cousin Vasily Romanzov, Nick's younger brother, who had become an Orthodox monk residing first at Point Reyes Station, California and then Manton near Lassen National Park. I could not have kept in close contact with them, or with my wider family without Peg's devoted engagement with them.

In these ways, and throughout our shared lives, Peg has been crucial in my recognizing, and celebrating my birth family through which I launched into my life abundant. My life has been more truly grace-filled thanks to love and encouragement, for which I am truly grateful. *Deo gratias!*

4

Brother

MY BROTHER GEORGE STEPHEN Dekar (September 16, 1949-February 18, 2003) had good health in his early years. At 6'4," he was an outstanding basketball player in high school. He played trumpet in the school band.

After his secondary education, George attended Diablo Valley Community College, where he continued to play basketball. After graduation, he attended the University of Washington in Seattle. His grades in engineering courses were good, and his grades in liberal arts classes were superlative. Especially skilled and precise in his drawings, George showed promise. Due to his encroaching illness, he graduated in 1971, a year later than would have normally been the case. His degree was in mechanical engineering.

For his first job, George moved to Texarkana, Arkansas. Shortly after starting this employment, George came to Chicago where I was studying. During this visit, earlier signs of schizophrenia became significantly more pronounced. George claimed his food was poisoned. Coming to understand that the onset of schizophrenia in young males often emerges between late teens and early twenties, Nancy and I acknowledged reality and tried to persuade my mother that George needed treatment. For some time, she resisted but finally sought medical care for him.

George received therapy with a number of doctors and facilities. He retired at a very young age and lived with mother the balance of her life. George often wandered around the neighborhood and stopped at a restaurant for breakfast. After our mother's death in 1999, George lived in group homes under care of a primary physician until his death in 2003.

Shortly thereafter, while preparing the family home for sale, Peg and I went through George's papers. We found that his health had declined during his university years more than we had known. While he had continued to attend classes, George's descent into mental illness had deepened.

In *Brother to a Dragonfly*, Baptist theologian and civil rights activist Will D. Campbell wrote of his love for his brother Joe. Campbell grieved Joe's death resulting from alcohol, drug, and other abuses but came to a fresh understanding of his brother's tragic life. In 1992, I met Campbell at the Roanoke, Virginia, BPFNA peace camp. I explained to him how his story helped me understand my deep anguish about George's mental illness. Signing my copy of his book *Providence*, he wrote, "For Paul, my brother, hope! Will Campbell."

After George's death, a policeman who had sometimes joined George for coffee attended a celebration of George's life. The officer characterized my brother as a gentle giant.

Reflecting on George's life, I recall playing endless board games, softball in our backyard, and basketball at nearby schools or parks. In part due to distance after I headed east to attend Colgate Rochester Divinity School (CRDS), I was saddened that I could not attend his basketball games, as I had early on.

As I complete introducing my birth family, I want to highlight my gratitude for having been raised in a loving family. Although we were not wealthy, there was always enough money to meet basic needs. As well, we enjoyed Sunday afternoon drives, camping, family gatherings, and vacations.

Holidays were special. In a Christmas 1948 photo, I sat with Santa Claus, full of expectation. We celebrated the birth of Jesus with good food, gifts, music and laughter on December 25 in the western Christian church and January 7 in the eastern Christian calendar during which we visited several relatives, including Genadie Stepanoff, whose tradition of decorating a tree with blue lights has become a permanent fixture of my family. Decades later at the start of Advent every year, Nancy and I visit a farm. We cut a tree and decorate it with blue lights. Similarly, we observed Easter twice.

We got our first television in the late 1950s. On one occasion, I recall sitting in a class at Las Lomas High School. I heard fire trucks pass by. Returning home, I was shocked to discover that our house had caught fire due to the telly's defective wiring.

My parents' household language with each other was Russian. Wanting to Americanize, they spoke English with Peg, George, and me. I learned some Russian and once sang a Russian-language song for which I was rewarded by being able to listen to a sporting event.[1]

Later, at the University of California, Berkeley, I took courses in Russian-language, history, politics and culture. Ever since, I have read books by Russian authors, watched movies based on Russian literature, and occasionally attended Russian Orthodox worship, especially at Easter.

As resources allowed, Dad and Mom helped sponsor additional relatives who had fled the Russian Revolution but remained in Eastern Europe for several years afterwards. Despite tensions, largely those owing to emotional wounds experienced from Mom's mother, my parents ensured that my siblings and I received a good education. Dad and Mom inculcated commitment to serve the greater common good and took enormous pride in our accomplishments. I am profoundly grateful. *Deo gratias!*

---

1. https://www.youtube.com/watch?v=bu9GX1n0A2w.

5

Nancy Jean Rose

IN THE FALL OF 1966, I was a second-year student at CRDS. Its curriculum required a practicum that entailed hands-on ministry. I served as assistant to Gordon Kurtz, then pastor of South Avenue Baptist Church. For Sunday worship I read scripture, led in prayer or, occasionally, preached. I also led a youth group.

One Sunday, a group of Genesee Hospital nursing students attended. I noticed a beautiful woman with long, dark hair. Nancy Jean Rose was in her third year studying to be a registered nurse. I called her, hoping for a date. She explained that she was already dating someone so she declined.

Was this the end of the story? No. Months later, one of Nancy's classmates, Jean Vastbinder, called. She thought Nancy might welcome a date. This time, Nancy accepted. Suite-mate Bill Northrup loaned me his Karmann Ghia, a two-person convertible Volkswagen for our first date.[1]

---

1. Finalizing *Life Abundant* in May 2025, I learned of Bill's death. I alerted a mutual friend Mahlon Gilbert who replied: Dear Paul, your news of Dear Bill comes ever so frequently these days as our Dear Ones bid farewell to us and to their earthly prominence. You and I have certainly had an intimate connection to Bill, stemming from the Universe's wisdom of joining you two as roomies. So many stirring conversations began in that dorm, as we were beginning our next chapters as men of faith, study, and personal awakening. I know how fortunate and safe Bill felt around you. So, naturally, in my conversation with Bill just a

Nancy and I fell in love. She continued to attend worship with me, often followed by a home-cooked meal. If another congregant did not invite us, the Kurtz family—Gordon, Melisse, Margaret (Peg), Elizabeth (Betsy), and four sons, Ted, Steve, Jim and John—always welcomed us. Without fail, Sunday's fare was pot roast, popcorn, and ice cream.

Rightly intuiting that our relationship was deepening, Gordon and Melisse nurtured our growing bonds and enthusiastically encouraged us to spend time together during the Spring of 1967. For example, Nancy and I enjoyed walking through Highland Park (a short distance between the seminary and church) during the spring when lilacs were in full bloom.

As Nancy talked of her nursing program, I became aware of her tremendous capacity to do more than simply provide medical care for patients. She affirmed, encouraged, and showed compassion even to those who were surly or uncooperative. I also sensed maternal qualities that would make Nancy a wonderful mother were she to have children.

Around the time of her graduation in the Spring of 1967, I drove to Montreal for a world's fair with Bill Northrup and two other CRDS students, Mahlon Gilbert and Eric Nelson. Upon return to Rochester, I was emboldened by their encouragement and proposed marriage. Nancy accepted.

As our relationship developed, I introduced Nancy to a relative, Svetlana Wishnakow, a niece of my grandfather Spira who had fled Russia after the Soviets came to power. Out came a bottle of vodka to toast my future wife. I still play a record, *Pianos in Paradise* with Ferrante and Teicher, gifted to me by Svetlana, "To dear Ricky as a remembrance from your cousin who will never forget you. Good luck!! Buena Suerte. Always, Svetlana."

---

few weeks ago, once more we reviewed those golden days. Bill came to my family's Ohio farm for my Ordination and to hear bro Kurtz preach that sermon. In that last telephone conversation, Bill recalled how he and I walked to his family gravesite on their farm, and how his presence there was going to feel just right. You've written of so many journeys you have walked in eight decades, and we both have grown from the faithful bosom confidence he shared with us. May he continue his Karmann Ghia ride, head high. Abiding love, Mahlon.

For the next six months, I lived in Virginia near Arlington Cemetery from which I walked across the Potomac River to Department of State offices for orientation and French language study prior to my first appointment in Cameroon. Nancy completed her nursing program and worked in one of the local hospitals where she had trained.

Due to distance, Nancy and I dated most regularly by phone. We often agreed to see the same movie and talk about it afterwards. Aware of my impending marriage, the Department of State interviewed several of Nancy's friends and required Nancy to provide a clean police record as a prerequisite to her receiving a diplomatic passport.

As able, I visited Nancy and met her family in the Ithaca, New York area. I discovered her love, and that of her family for an area that brims with beautiful waterfalls, lakes, and farmland. During these brief times together, we explored the region, both around her home and nearer to Rochester where Letchworth State Park along the Genesee River Valley was aflame with color that Fall.

We married on December 31, 1967 at Nancy's home congregation in Danby, near Ithaca. Mahlon Gilbert and Gordon Kurtz co-officiated. My family came from California, with my brother George serving as best man and my sister Peg as part of the wedding party. Nancy's sister Lynda and brother Jimmy were also members of the wedding party. Nancy's nursing school friends Nancy Bernreuther and Jean Vastbinder were maid of honor and matron. Bill Northrup and Eric Nelson served as ushers.

Friends for whom Nancy had baby-sat contributed to the celebration in several ways. Fran Helbig defrayed expenses. Lou Bowles sang. Good weather prevailed for guests traveling to Ithaca. However, a snowstorm hampered their return travel.

After the wedding ceremony, Nancy and I drove south to York, near Harrisburg, Pennsylvania. In the morning, snow blanketed our car, which now had a flat tire. I changed the tire. We had bad luck and had a second flat. I again changed the tire, and we successfully reached Washington D. C. where Nancy received her diplomatic passport. We then proceeded to New York City for the start of our honeymoon.

A few days later, January 5th, we sailed to France on the Queen Elizabeth II. Since the ship was half-empty and we were newlyweds, we were given a first-class cabin. We enjoyed the start of our marriage in spite of sea sickness during the crossing and a bout of flu in Paris, France.

Departing the US for almost three years, Nancy and I began our life together without having to navigate relations with our birth families, friends, or relatives. Neither did we have to deal with my mother's disapproval of my choice for a wife, or that of her mother. Margaret thought Nancy's family did not have the economic means or social stature to have warranted her becoming my wife.

By contrast, my father expressed great confidence in my choice of a spouse. My siblings also supported us. My sister visited us in Cameroon. She and her husband Stacy consistently have demonstrated their love for us.

Before we were married, Nancy was already a registered nurse. During our time in Cameroon, she served as embassy nurse when needed. On one occasion, she accompanied a former Peace Corps volunteer back home due to serious injuries in an accident. Nancy also provided an English-language nursery for several children in our Cameroon home. She took French-language classes to improve her ability to communicate in both official languages of our host country. Despite having household help, Nancy did most of the cooking and became a magnificent hostess, a major role in diplomatic life. These were tangible ways by which she supported my career.

As our assignment to Cameroon approached its end, Nancy and I wrestled with the decision to remain or resign from the US Department of State. A key consideration was family. Nancy and I wanted children. Though the government took family into account when making assignments, we recognized the challenge of raising children when we had to move to new posts every few years.

I initially opted to take a leave of absence for a year. Returning to Rochester, Nancy resumed her nursing career while I completed my seminary studies. We then returned to Washington, where Nancy again found a nursing position. I served as assistant to Deputy Secretary of State, Alan Anderson Reich in the Bureau of Educational and Cultural Affairs and was informed that my next assignment would be in Europe.

Nancy was very helpful as I wrestled with having to choose between remaining in what was a dreamed-for career or resigning to an uncertain future. Learning to depend on her wisdom, I found Nancy encouraging as the path we chose was for me to resign and to attend graduate school at the University of Chicago.

During my doctoral studies in Chicago, we lived at the Piccadilly, which opened in 1927 as a fourteen-story hotel about a mile from the University, which had purchased and converted the facility to student housing. Nancy found part-time employment both before and after the birth of Nathaniel on December 27, 1971. For the next few years, Nancy focused on raising Nathaniel. As an advantage of living in student housing, we were part of a cooperative through which we exchanged baby sitting with several couples.

Nancy took a religious studies course at Roosevelt University's downtown Chicago campus with Tom Sinclair Faulker, another student in the Divinity School. This was the start of a long friendship with Tom. On one occasion, Tom broke a leg with the result that Nancy had to transport him to Roosevelt for the session of the course that she was auditing.

As I neared completion of my doctoral program, we moved to Mount Pleasant, Michigan where I began my teaching career at Central Michigan University during the 1975–1976 academic year. Nancy, Nathaniel and I enjoyed exploring the region. The summer of 1976, I completed revisions of my thesis.

I then accepted a position as professor at McMaster University in Hamilton, Ontario, Canada, where our second son, Matthew, was born on April 16, 1979. Nancy concentrated on raising family. As she met both sons after school, Nancy developed a strong network of friends among other parents. She especially enjoyed organizing birthday parties and welcoming the closest friends of Nathaniel and Matthew into our home. She maintained a little black book, with dates of births, deaths, and other significant moments and continues to remind me monthly of significant events.

In the early 1980s, Nancy took a refresher course at Mohawk College in Hamilton and resumed her nursing career part-time with the Victorian Order of Nurses, which provides nursing services through in-home visitation. She thus augmented our family income.

Over my teaching career, Nancy has always been supportive. When developing a paper, sermon, article, or book, I read the text to her, or she reads the manuscript and afterwards gives detailed comments and important critique. Drawing on her experience as a diplomat's wife, Nancy has entertained countless students and friends as well as her former nursing colleagues.

During each of four sabbaticals that punctuated my teaching years, Nancy found an important niche. During 1982–1983, we lived at an ecumenical institute midway between Jerusalem and Bethlehem in the Holy Land. Nancy helped at an orphanage in Bethlehem.

Living in Oxford during the 1991–1992 academic year, Nancy volunteered at a women's shelter. Returning to Hamilton, she drew on this experience and became involved with Interval House, which provides emergency shelter, safety, planning, and support services for women with or without children that have experienced abuse or violence.

As Nancy helped women and their children fleeing abuse, she discerned a need of many women for support beyond their initial time at emergency shelters. Nancy joined a group that included members of our congregation, MacNeill Baptist Church, and of other congregations to raise funds for a second-stage housing project. Many nights of bingo, writing grant applications, and appealing for political support resulted in successful fund-raising and the establishment of Phoenix Place, a second-stage, five-unit century-old home house in a confidential location in Hamilton.

Phoenix Place offers a safe refuge for families. Residents receive trauma-informed individual and group counseling, housing support, appointment accompaniment, legal referral, safety planning, children's counselling referrals, and client advocacy. Women and their families are able to reside at Phoenix Place for up to one year while they await transition to permanent, safe, and affordable housing. Now administered by the Young Women's Christian Association, Phoenix Place continues to assist women and their children in transition.[2]

During our third sabbatical, one term in 1998, we lived at Whitley College of the Melbourne University in Australia, our first of what proved to be the eight sojourns there. We met members of a new monastic community affiliated with the Baptist Union of Victoria, the Community of the Transfiguration. Nancy found the community an inspiring source of hope for the world at a time of spiritual, social, and ecological crisis. During subsequent visits to Australia, we spent some time at the monastery. July 8, 2005, we became part of its "greater community." Community members especially valued Nancy for her gifts of hospitality and clarity of wisdom.

Our fourth sabbatical involved two locations. During the Fall 2002 term, I resided at a Church of the Brethren institution, Elizabethtown College in Lancaster County, Pennsylvania. Nancy remained in Memphis where son Matthew was completing his studies at Rhodes College. Again, Nancy's nursing career augmented our family income.

During the Winter-Spring term in early 2003, we resided at St. Johns Abbey in Collegeville, Minnesota. The monastery came to our attention through reading *The Cloister Walk* by Kathleen Norris. During our residence, Nancy volunteered with Sisters of the Order of Saint Benedict, at St. Joseph where Nancy helped the nuns in a variety of ways.

During our time in Minnesota, Nancy and I enjoyed exploring the state, for example driving to Lake Itasca, source of the Mississippi River. Nancy also enjoyed walking along Fruit Farm Road where she saw llamas, sheep, blue birds, and other forest life.

Nancy experienced great pain when learning of the murder, April 24, 2003, of Memphis colleague Mary Jane Cruchon. A nurse to elderly patients, Mary Jane was looking after a resident in her

2. https://www.ywcahamilton.org/housing/phoenix-place/.

High Point Terrace neighborhood when a paroled ex-prisoner killed her.

In early 2006, living in Memphis, Nancy responded to a need to help our son Nathaniel and his wife Jackie to care for our granddaughters Abbey and Emma. Recalling how supportive Nancy had been in my career, I affirmed this opportunity for Nancy to assume a significant responsibility for their after-school activities. As well as providing Abbey and Emma wonderful nurture, Nancy re-connected with nursing colleagues and volunteers with whom she had shared in developing Phoenix Place.

In retirement, Nancy walks for exercise, reads prodigiously, serves in various roles with our spiritual community, and loves our cottage time. Nancy grounds me because she is practical and checks my idealistic and sometimes impractical tendencies. She has a great sense of humor. She provides wise counsel for colleagues, family, and friends. She has been the glue that has held me, our family, and many friends together.

The Lebanese writer Kahlil Gibran describes the love I have experienced from Nancy in *The Prophet*, a copy of which I gave her years ago. I highlighted the words: "Love gives naught but itself and takes naught from itself. Love possesses not nor would it be possessed. . . . Love has no other desire but to fulfil itself. . . . let these be your desires, to melt and be like a running brook that sings its melody to the night . . . And then to sleep with a prayer for the beloved in your heart and a song of praise upon your lips."[3]

In 2017, for our fiftieth wedding anniversary, Nancy and I gathered with our sons and their families at Hilton Head in South Carolina. We celebrated fifty years of shared growth and looked forward to deepening our love. Nancy has been my best friend and coequal partner for nearly sixty years, sharing deeply in our lives of abundance and grace. Nancy is the heart of my life abundant. *Deo gratias!*

---

3. Gibran, *Prophet*, 14–15.

6

Nathaniel and Family

DURING OUR FIRST MONTHS in Chicago, Nancy and I had expected the birth of our child on Christmas Day. We chose Nathaniel, a Hebrew word meaning gift of God as a name. While he tarried two days and was born December 27, 1971, we have always considered him a gift of the Holy One.

In September 1976, we moved to Hamilton, Ontario. Nancy and I enrolled Nathaniel in French immersion Kindergarten at Earl Kitchener School. We wanted him to be able to communicate in Canada's two official languages.

After initially renting for a year, we purchased a home at 29 Bruce Street, Hamilton. It was near Earl Kitchener as well as Ryerson Middle School,[1] where Nathaniel was able to continue in the French immersion program as also at Westdale Secondary School. In addition to thriving in academics, Nathaniel was an outstanding athlete in basketball and curling.

1. In the nineteenth century, Egerton Ryerson, a Methodist minister, was a prominent contributor to the design of the Ontario public school system. The residential school system, a network of boarding schools for indigenous peoples created to isolate indigenous children from the influence of their own culture and religion and to assimilate them into the dominant Euro-Canadian culture has come under scrutiny. In June 2022, trustees with the Hamilton-Wentworth District School Board settled on Kanétskare Elementary as a replacement name for this school.

Nathaniel continued his bilingual education uninterrupted during my sabbatical leave in Jerusalem, 1982–1983. Nathaniel took a bus into the city for courses in French at an international school.

From 1989–1993, Nathaniel attended the University of Waterloo. During my Oxford sabbatical, 1991–1992, Nathaniel remained in our Canadian home and visited us both at Christmas, and at the end of the academic year after which our family traveled through France.

After Nathaniel graduated in kinesiology, he continued his education in sports injury management at the Oakville campus of Sheridan College. A feature of the program was the availability of internships, one of which led to employment after he graduated in 1996. Nathaniel then sought credentials with the Canadian Athletic Therapist Association and has subsequently worked professionally in the field. He has also continued to play baseball and other sports. He successfully completed a triathlon and other sporting events.

In December 1999, I solemnized the wedding of Nathaniel and Jacqueline Jennifer Miller. A graduate of McMaster University, Jackie has been not only a wonderful partner for Nathaniel, but also a blessing in Nancy and my lives. In part because Jackie's mother Gaye had had a stroke when Jackie was eleven years old, Jackie developed a very close relationship with Nancy. Nancy and I enjoy her outgoing personality and turn to Jackie for her professional skills in such areas as finance, management, and navigating the Internet.

In 2000, Nathaniel and Jackie moved to San Francisco. They stayed long enough to have a daughter before returning to Canada. Abigail Jack-Ellen Dekar was born on May 23, 2001 at the same San Francisco clinic of Stanford University where I had been born.

Abbey was an excellent student through her primary and secondary school education. She won scholarships during her studies at the University of Guelph. She initially lived on campus and enrolled in a co-op program though which she gained work experience, developed skills essential for her a future career as a chartered accountant, and earned money, some of which she saved in order to travel in Switzerland and England after graduation.

During and after the 2020–2021 Covid-19 pandemic, Abbey continued her studies from home. Subsequently, most of her university education was on-line, accessed from home. Abbey graduated in the spring of 2024. She quickly found employment with a local (Ancaster) accounting firm. At the time of writing, Abbey is studying for Chartered Professional Accountant accreditation.

For many years, Abbey has played soccer. A skilled defender and a super soccer aficionada, she has been an outstanding member of several championship teams. Through the years, Nancy and I have watched many of her games.

Nathaniel and Jackie's second daughter, Emma Jessamine Dekar, was born on June 18, 2004, in Hamilton. Like her sister, Emma was an excellent student through her primary and secondary school education and won scholarships during her studies at Trent University, from which she expects to graduate in 2026.

In the summer of 2024, Emma worked at a conservation area and developed expertise with invertebrates. For the summer of 2025, she secured a similar position that will serve her well in her professional life. In her extra-curricular activities, Emma has thrived in basketball, volleyball, and sketching. As with her sister, Nancy and I have watched many of Emma's games, and celebrated when her basketball team won city championship.

Nathaniel currently assesses health insurance claims for Manulife, an international services group that provides financial advice, insurance, and asset management for individuals, groups and institutions. Jackie works in the healthcare industry with Point Click Care, an internet cloud-based platform that connects health services and financial operations. Since the 2020–2021 Covid-19 pandemic, Nathaniel and Jackie have worked primarily from their Hamilton home.

Early in my academic career, I made a point of attending conferences during which I often offered papers. Perhaps my major professional associations met between Christmas and the New Year. It was not long before I realized that such travel, and the preparation of presentations deprived me of family time during the week between Nathaniel's birthday and Nancy and my anniversary. To enjoy family time, I stopped attending those sessions.

Since returning to Hamilton from Memphis in 2008, during the last week of the year, Nancy and I enjoy a week with Nathaniel and his family, joined when possible with Matthew and his family, at a resort generally a short driving distance from Hamilton. This has been one way we have been able to appreciate family time together in a beautiful setting. In a very real way, these weekly, end-of year holidays together have been an essential dimension of our shared lives of abundance, for which I can only exclaim, *Deo gratias!*

7

Matthew and Family

OUR SECOND SON, MATTHEW Paul, was born April 16, 1979. When it came time for him to begin his formal education, we enrolled him in French immersion, as was the case with his brother. During my sabbatical leaves, Matthew was able to continue his bilingual education. During our first sabbatical, in Israel, Matthew attended a nursery run by the Lutheran Church. During our second sabbatical, in England, Matthew attended an international school in which many courses were taught in French. During our third sabbatical, in Australia, Matthew enrolled in courses at Melbourne University for which he received credit at Rhodes College in Memphis, Tennessee where he majored in biology.

Like his brother, Matthew thrived academically. In 1992, for example, shortly after we returned from England, we received a call from the principal of Earl Kitchener School and learned of a "problem." Matthew's French-language skills had improved so much during his year in a European context, that he was able to skip a grade.

During his high school education, Matthew played Canadian-rules football. In Australia, he learned to play Aussie-rules football, or "footie." In addition, he learned to play rugby, a sport he continued at Rhodes College, a Presbyterian-related institution in Memphis. His team sometimes played against teams from much larger institutions such as the University of Alabama. A tradition at Rhodes, was to ask an ordained parent of one of the graduands to offer a commencement blessing. As a result, I offered a prayer during Matthew's graduation ceremony.

Matthew continued on to graduate school at the Fayetteville campus of the University of Arkansas from which he received a Master of Science and a Ph.D. in aquatic ecology. After a brief period in which he worked in Canada, he continued his formal education as a post-doctoral research fellow and lecturer in the Department of Biology at Baylor University in Waco, Texas.

Throughout these years, Matthew found summer employment in various settings, including Alaska, Colorado, and Ohio. While this did not provide substantial income, he did gain invaluable experience.

Matthew met Melissa Dudley in Waco. A graduate of Shorter University in Atlanta, Georgia, Melissa was an environmental scientist working as a pollution biologist for the Texas Parks and Wildlife Department. Nancy and I quickly discerned her warm personality and professional gifts. When I was asked to officiate at Matt and Melissa's wedding on August 25, 2012, to be celebrated on a beach in Alabama along the Gulf of Mexico, I expressed concern about hurricane season. We enjoyed the celebration and fortunately were able to depart before a major storm hit the area.

Matthew and Melissa initially settled in Elk Grove, California where they both worked for the US government. In part for the opportunity to live closer to Melissa's parents and five siblings Matthew and Melissa moved in 2017 to Atlanta where they continued doing crucial environmental work. After four years, they returned to California and, at the time of writing, live in Folsom, near Sacramento. Matthew is Director of the Western Ecological Research Centre for the US Geological Survey. Melissa is a Supervisory Natural Resources Specialist assessing environmental compliance for water infrastructure projects for the Department of the Interior.

On August 19, 2014, Matthew and Melissa's first child, Drake Matthew, was born. Their second child, Nadine Camille was born July 4, 2016. In choosing where to live, Matthew and

Melissa have researched schools and other amenities favorable to raising Drake and Nadine. Both have prospered in elementary school since the family moved to Folsom, California. At the time of writing, Drake is in grade 5, Nadine in grade 3. Each has served on their school council. Both have thrived in various sports, with downhill skiing a current passion. Their home is just over an hour's drive from ski slopes.

Having studied fish biology and management with specialists across the country, Matthew has had a successful career with the US Fish and Wildlife Service and US Geological Survey both within the Department of the Interior. When Matthew's education and employment led him to reside permanently in the US, Nancy was able to spend significant time in California helping Matthew and Melissa with Drake and Nadine. While geography makes it impossible for Nancy and me to connect with them in person as regularly as is the case with Nathaniel and his family, we talk almost every week by Zoom, a half-hour conversation during which we catch up on everyone's news.

To conclude this introduction to our family, I highlight how blessed Nancy and I have been throughout our marriage. Graced by the love of every family member, we celebrate each one's gifts, friendship, and wide network of relationships. Especially important was our decision to retire early and return to southern Ontario where Nancy and I could deepen our ties our sons and their families. Our lives could not be blessed more abundantly. *Deo gratias*!

8

Russian Orthodox Religious Roots

I WAS BAPTIZED AS an infant in the Russian Orthodox Church of Saint Nicholas in downtown San Francisco where my father had worshipped. At the time, my parents lived near the Fleishhacker Zoo a few blocks from the Pacific Ocean. When we moved to Walnut Creek, we did not find a Russian Orthodox church. We initially attended a Methodist church and, subsequently, Valley Baptist Church (now Shell Ridge Community Church).

While I have never returned to regular Russian Orthodox worship, I occasionally attend the Orthodox Easter service as a crucial part of my heritage and sense of abundant life. Shortly after midnight on Sunday morning the congregation moves outside and circles the host church three times. Expectantly, the priest comes out of the church and announces to the people that Christ is risen. The people respond, "Truly He is risen." And all chant, "Christ is risen from the dead, trampling down death by death, and on those in the tombs bestowing life."

While attending worship, I cross myself in the distinctive manner of Orthodox Christians. Despite my limited Russian language facility, I carry a copy of the liturgy. This enables me to follow the liturgy and recite the prayers. I have also gone on retreat at several Orthodox monasteries, including Mt. Sinai in Egypt and Mt. Athos in Greece where there is a Russian Orthodox monastery.

Russian Orthodox Religious Roots

I have done retreats at several Orthodox communities, including the Monastery of St. John of Shanghai and San Francisco of which my cousin Vasily Romanzov was a priest. Once located at Point Reyes Station, California, the monastery moved in June 2006 to forty-two acres of Ponderosa forest in Manton near the foothills of Mt. Lassen National Park.[1] In 2011, my sister Peg and I visited the community. I had planned to return in 2023 but learned of Vasily's death in early June. His death was unexpected. Peg and Stacy rented a car and drove to Manton for the funeral. At a celebration of his life, Vasily's daughter Kita spoke as follows,

> When I was five years old and my father left for the monastery, my mother convinced me that it is normal for fathers to leave their families and go to be at a monastery once their children are at least five years old. She relayed that she always had a father in her life, he came for every birthday and every special event. And she is very happy that he now has fulfilled his dream of being with Jesus.

In Combermere, Ontario, I have done three week-long retreats at Madonna House, which draws on the Russian Orthodox spirituality of co-founder Catharine de Hueck Doherty. In my daily journal, I carry the "little mandate" of the community. It reads as follows,

> Arise — go! Sell all you possess. Give it directly, personally to the poor. Take up my cross (their cross) and follow me, going to the poor, being poor, being one with them, one with me. Little — be always little . . . simple, poor, childlike. Preach the gospel *with your life, without compromise*. Listen to the Spirit. He will lead you. Do little things exceedingly well for love of me. Love. . . love. . . love, never counting the cost. Go into the marketplace and stay with me. Pray, fast. Pray always, fast. Be hidden. Be a light to your neighbor's feet. Go without fears into the depth of men's hearts. I shall be with you. Pray always. *I will be your rest.*[2]

---

1. https://monasteryofstjohn.org/ for information about the monastery.
2. Doherty, *Poustinia*, 204, and *Essential Writings*, 126–7, emphasis in text. For prayers from the community, *The Complete Rosary, Divine Mercy Chaplet*

Life Abundant

I sometimes listen to a recording of liturgical music from Madonna House, or a c. d. of contemplative prayer with Jesus Prayer, which goes as follows, "O Lord Jesus Christ, have mercy on me, a sinner." Another prayer reads, "O Heavenly King, O Comforter, the Spirit of truth, which art in all places and fillest all things, the treasure of blessings, and giver of life, come and abide in us. Cleanse us from all impurity, and of thy goodness save our souls."[3]

By such prayers, I honor my Russian Orthodox spiritual roots, foundational to my early life and ongoing sense of being a beloved son of God. In turn, I have sought to nurture in others, individually and collectively, the spiritual practices that have contributed to my of life abundant.

---

and Jesus Prayer is a wonderful resource used in a talk at a Thomas Merton session: "Praying in the Way of Catherine de Hueck Doherty and Thomas Merton," *Merton Seasonal* 48/3 (Fall 2023) 23–26.

3. *Eastern Orthodox Prayers*, 2 and 24.

9

Jewish Religious Roots

GIVEN MY EARLY UPBRINGING in the Russian Orthodox Church, I had no early awareness of my Jewish religious roots. Around 1952, I accompanied grandmother Margaret to Vancouver, British Colombia, Canada. We went there to meet her brother David Burstein (1906–1993) and his family who had recently arrived in North America.

David's father, Gregory Burstein (1819–1912) was eighty-seven when David was born. His mother, Eve Kushner Burstein (1870–1937) was fifty years younger. Why the age difference? Gregory had married previously. After his first wife's death, he focused on a fur trading business. Eve had two brothers, both rabbis. She was married and went from Siberia to Ukraine to visit her sick brother. When she returned, her husband was living with another Russian girl. Her brothers confronted him: "You have to divorce your wife. We're going to drown you in the river. You have to marry our sister."

He refused to abandon his mistress. This freed Eve to divorce him and marry Gregory Burstein with whom she expected a short marriage. Successful in business, Gregory bought pelts—squirrels especially—from peasants. Eve had a special loom from floor to ceiling.. Salespeople came from all over from Russia to buy furs and other accessories that were shipped to Leipzig, Germany to be dried, cured, dyed, and prepared for finishing. The business provided stability and a comfortable life.

Gregary and Eve had four children: Margaret, Leah, Katya, and David, youngest of the four. David was born on April 16, 1906. My mother Ariadne was among those who attended his Bar Mitzvah. At the age of eighteen, David's mother was concerned her son would be conscripted into the Soviet army, so she acquired papers for him changing his birth date. He left home and off he went by train to Harbin, Manchuria where he worked odd jobs. Uncle David put himself through dental school with financial support from a local Jewish organization and his sister Margaret, my maternal grandmother who by then lived in Seattle, Washington.

For a period during the First World War, Margaret, David's oldest sibling, lived in Kiev along with her husband Spiradon (Spira) and daughter Ariadne (my mother). As the Communist regime consolidated power, Spira, Margaret, and Ada fled, first to Harbin where Spira found employment as an engineer. and then to the US. Around 1926, they were able to get a visa to immigrate to the US. Grandmother worked for over seventeen years in a laundry, the last four as shop foreman. Five cents an hour. In her first letter to her brother, David, Margaret wrote, "This [America] is paradise; sell the house, and try to get to China and then come to the US."

David's other sisters were Leah and Katya. Leah remained in Siberia. She studied medicine at Tomsk Polytechnic University and became a doctor after graduating around 1926. She and her husband Vladimir Simkin and had two daughters, Ina and Irene. Early during the Second World War, Leah and her younger daughter Ina fled to Brest-Litovsk on the Polish border. They died in the Holocaust.

Katya, David's third sister, married a Yugoslav lawyer named Gero. In 1922 they fled from Russia to Yugoslavia where she became a secondary school teacher and had three children. I met her when she visited her North American family.

In 1932, David met and married Olga Kotovich who was from Vilnius, Poland before its annexation by the Soviet Union

Jewish Religious Roots

during World War II.[1] An older brother of Olga was murdered by drowning in a well with graffiti smeared on their home, "Kikes get out of Russia." Due to anti-Jewish pogroms, Olga moved with her family to Irkutsk in Siberia where she met David. After the Revolution they fled to Shanghai where David practiced dentistry in their apartment.

David and Olga had one daughter. Eva was born on December 8, 1941, when Japan bombed Pearl Harbor.[2] In 1948 when the Chinese Communists came to power, David realized Jews were no longer safe in Shanghai. With the goal of reuniting with his sister Margaret, David sought to immigrate to the US. At the time, however, immigration of Jews to the US proved to be impossible. David's next initiative was successful. The family obtained a visa and moved to British Colombia, Canada where David provided isolated First Nations people dental services.

Around 1952, the family moved to San Francisco. David opened a dental lab. I had fairly regular contact with them and became more aware of my Jewish heritage. I called Uncle David during the Six-day War between Israel and several Arab countries in June 1967 to ask if he thought "we Jews" would survive.

Eva and I developed a life-long friendship. During an interview in May 2011 when Eve and her husband Gordon visited in Dundas, Eva recalled taking me to a Conservative synagogue in San Francisco. The Rabbi was cold and traditional. Eva felt uncomfortable for me because the sermon, mostly in Hebrew, was boring, over our heads, and irrelevant to contemporary problems.

Eva was fluent in several languages, including Russian and modern Hebrew, which proved especially helpful when, in 2014, I accompanied Eva and her husband. Gordon to visit Israel. We stayed with relatives and toured sites deemed holy by adherents of all three Abrahamic religions.

---

1. After that war, Vilnius became capital of the Lithuanian Soviet Socialist Republic. It is now an independent state.

2. December 8 because she was on the other side of the international dateline.

Eva was also fluent in French. We sometimes spoke French, which I was studying in High School. Eve and I often visited Chinatown or other city attraction. One highpoint was City Lights Bookstore, now a historic landmark, where I purchased some of the first books in my personal library, including copies of Rachel Carson's *Silent Spring* (New York, 1962) and Thomas Merton's selection from the writings of Mahatma Gandhi, *Gandhi on Non-Violence* (New York, 1964).

Eva decided that I should learn to dance. On one occasion, we had dinner at the Tonga Room of the Fairmont Hotel, atop Nob Hill in San Francisco. The ambiance was beautiful. And there, Eva taught me to dance.

Over the years, I have used a Jewish prayerbook gifted to me by Eva. When I attend Jewish worship, I don a *kippah* (Hebrew word for the skullcap traditionally worn by Jewish men) that Eva also gifted to me along with a *mezuzah* (Hebrew for doorpost) that graces a doorway in our home. Its inscription quotes the Shema "Hear, O Israel: The Lord is our God, the Lord alone. You shall love the Lord your God with all your heart and with all your soul and with all your might" (Deuteronomy 6:4–5), the central prayer of Judaism.

In 1981, I was on a Holy Land study tour that I co-led with Mel Hillmer. Mel taught New Testament at McMaster Divinity College and was its Principal for ten years. The trip enabled me to finalize arrangements for a sabbatical for the 1982–1983 academic year. My family lived at Tantur, an ecumenical center on the Jerusalem-Bethlehem road. My primary research concerned the Israel-Palestine conflict. I interviewed widely and took courses in the English-language program of Hebrew University. In 1985, with support of a study grant, I returned to Israel and continued research and writing focused on Israeli-Palestinian peace initiatives.

These trips contributed to my teaching in McMaster University's peace studies program. As well, I published several articles about the Israel-Palestine conflict and Christian-Jewish relations. One article focused on the legacy of Morris Zeidman, a Polish-born Jew who immigrated to Canada at age sixteen. Drawn to

Jewish Religious Roots

a Christian Synagogue by a Yiddish sign as the House of Good Tidings of the Messiah of the Children of Israel, he converted to Christianity and supported Jews fleeing persecution to come to North America.[3]

I developed a relationship with the family of Morris Zeidman. After his death, his son Alex Zeidman approached me about the disposition of Morris Zeidman's library. I recognized it contained exceptionally important documents, especially in Yiddish. At the time, Nancy and I were friends with neighbours, Adele Reinhartz who at the time taught Jewish studies at McMaster, and her husband Barry Walfish, Judaica specialist at the University of Toronto. I put Barry in touch with the Zeidman family, with the result that the collection found an apt home.

In my role as a chaplain at McMaster University, I organized daily worship in the campus chapel. Every year in April, I led a Yom HaShoah service as a memorial to six million Jews and others slaughtered by the Nazis between 1933 and 1945, including several of my relatives. I occasionally taught an introductory course in religion with a unit on Judaism.

In 1994 when I interviewed for a position at Memphis Theological Seminary of the Cumberland Presbyterian Church, I replied a question about books that had shaped my theology and spirituality. Among others, I named two by Jews as formative, Martin Buber's *I and Thou* and Simon Weil's *Waiting for God*.

As Nancy and I prepared to move to Memphis, our neighbors, Barry and Adele, alerted the newly appointed rabbi of their synagogue of the availability of our home, which the rabbi bought. To the dismay of Nancy and myself, a neighbor criticized us for selling our home to Jews. This recalled a time when Jews could only purchase homes in Westdale, the neighborhood around McMaster University.

From 2018–2024, I represented Canadian Quakers on the Christian Interfaith Reference Group (CIRG) of the Canadian Council of Churches (CCC). CIRG was formed to explore new

---

3. I share the story in "From Jewish Mission to Inner City Mission: The Scott Mission and Its Antecedents in Toronto, 1908 to 1964," in *Canadian Protestant and Catholic Missions . . . Essays in Honour of John Webster Grant*.

spiritual and theological territory demanded by living in a pluralistic society.

On November 16–17, 2022, we had a powerful time for reflection and lament on the loss of a national multilateral forum for Christian-Jewish dialogue. In terms of my contribution, I stressed throughout the process the importance of listening and forming relationships, which I knew might prove difficult given the history of Christian-Jewish relations.

In addition to occasional opportunities to speak or write about my Jewish roots, I serve on the Israel Palestine Working Group of the Canadian Friends Service Committee. Among recent initiatives, we have called for Canada to end its military relationship with all states, including Israel, that may use Canadian arms to violate basic human rights.

Finally, I have mentored some Jewish students, including John M. Kaplan. At the time he studied at MTS, John served as cantor of a Memphis synagogue. In addition to his M. A. thesis on trends in worship reflected in a North American Reform Jewish Congregation, John initiated an important dialogue between the Jewish and Palestinian communities in the Memphis area.

During my retirement party from MTS, John offered a prayer, as did a Muslim community leader, Dr. Nabil Bayakly who at time directed a community center in Memphis. By inviting them, the seminary recognized my Jewish roots and interfaith commitment, crucial aspects of my life abundant.

Writing in mid-2025, I am grieved by growing antisemitism, hostility to "the other," and so-called "white nationalism, in the United States, Australia, Canada, and elsewhere. Attacks on the worship space of various religious communities, assaults on people wearing the religious garb of their communities, and gun battles between various gangs have become all too frequent. My prayer is that this chapter highlighting my Jewish roots stirs action to nurture and deepen interfaith understanding, a crucial aspect of my life abundant and a necessary element of healing at a time of growing polarization in Canada and elsewhere.

10

The Arts

MUSIC HAS ALWAYS PLAYED a wonderful part in my life. When I was growing up, two pieces of furniture were prominent in our home, a radio on which I listened to songs of virtually every genre, and a spinet or console piano.

My musical education was intermittent. Throughout my primary school years, my sister and I took piano lessons with Helen E. Grout. She lived in Pleasant Hill, the town adjacent to Walnut Creek. Mother drove us to lessons. At school, our brother George played a brass instrument.

Mrs. Grout organized recitals at the end of each school year for which we memorized pieces. One concert took place at the Chapel of the Chimes in Oakland on May 31, 1959. I accompanied a trumpeter who played the *Star-Spangled Banner*. I also played several solo pieces during the recital: *Rustles of Spring* by the Norwegian composer Christian August Sinding; *Anitra's Dance*, an excerpt from the *Peer Gynt Suite* by Edvard Grieg, another Norwegian composer; and *Moonlight Sonata* by the German composer Ludwig van Beethoven. Judy Arnold and I performed a duet, Franz Suppe's *Poet and Peasant Overture*. My sister also played pieces.

I stopped piano lessons when I began secondary school. Later while studying at CRDS, I took organ lessons for two years and practiced on the seminary organ. I have continued to play on a

Life Abundant

nineteenth-century pump organ owned for several generations by Nancy's family. She took lessons and played it in her youth.

When Nancy and I settled in Hamilton, Ontario, Arlene Wright was pianist with the Hamilton Philharmonic Orchestra and McMaster University's Department of Music. She gave lessons in an auditorium across from my office at McMaster Divinity College. At some point, we purchased one of her pianos, later donated to our Quaker meeting to accompany Christmas caroling and on other occasions. I join my Quaker community when we visit shut-ins and sing Christmas carols. I sometimes visit the Meeting House when no one else is there to play on it and sing alone.

I sing solo because I cannot carry a tune in a group. I remember being excused from singing in a high school concert. Similarly in 1992, when I participated in a BPFNA conference at La Boquita, Nicaragua, I joined other delegates in attending worship at First Baptist at Managua. Gustavo Parajón was pastor. His wife Joan, an accomplished musician, was choir director.[1] She invited our group to sing with the choir. During practice, Joan heard something amiss. Pointing in my direction, she asked me to sing. I did. She dismissed me.

On another occasion, a chapel service at McMaster Divinity College, I sat next to a student, Chris Vanderwater, who laughed. "Why?" I asked. He replied that he was aware of my reputation. Continuing, he added, "You really can't sing."

Nevertheless, music contributes enormously to abundance in my life. I love choral music. I listen regularly to a Sunday morning Canadian Broadcasting Corporation radio program entitled Choral Concert. I attend concerts given by local choirs. Several times a year, Nancy and I attend the Hamilton Philharmonic Orchestra. When they are joined by the Bach Elgar Choir or a youth choir, I sing along, *sotto voce*, in a quiet voice.

---

1. In *Healing the World. Gustavo Parajón, Public Health and Peacemaking Pioneer*, Butry and Albuquerque write about this remarkable couple. I describe them in "Martin Luther King, Jr. and Nonviolent Justice Seekers in Latin America and the Caribbean," *Nonviolence for the Third Millennium*, ed. Harak, 137–54. The government has closed the church; https://www.christianpost.com/news/nicaragua-evangelical-and-protestant-churches-lose-legal-status.html.

The Arts

In terms of other arts, in high school, I occasionally had a role performing in plays. Later, during my McMaster Divinity College years, Linda Watson-Burgess and Heather Duff were among members of the student body. In addition to being outstanding students, both had experience directing and sometimes writing plays. Over a number of years, I joined a drama group that they led. We did readings and performed plays at various churches. Although my experience in music and theatre has been limited, attending these performing arts remains a central element of my life abundant.

11

My Friend Russ

MY FAMILY MOVED TO Walnut Creek during second or third grade. We lived at 1929 Meadow Road next to Russ Beeson and his mother Della. Russ had been an antique-car aficionado and sports car racer until he fell victim to a crippling disease, polio, just prior to March 26, 1953, when medical researcher Jonas Salk announced he has successfully tested a vaccine against the virus.

Despite his confinement to bed and iron lung, Russ read widely flipping pages with a rubber-tipped stick in his mouth. He instructed his nursing attendants how to restore antique furnishings that he entered into competition for the Walnut Festival that has occurred mid-September for nearly ninety years.

Russ was an advocate for disability rights. In the early 1960s, he supported the efforts of another polio victim, Ed Roberts, to enroll at the University of California, Berkeley. His admission was rejected. Such advocacy took place at a time when Independent Living Movement was emerging.

Early in our friendship, Russ asked me to play Santa Claus for family Christmas gatherings. For several years, I donned a beard and outfit. Finally, my cover was blown when one of Russ' relatives exclaimed, "That's not Santa Claus. That's Ricky."

My grandfather Spira Dovjenko regularly visited our family in Walnut Creek. Once, early in our years living next to Russ, a police car came by. Worried that there had been a Soviet invasion during a time of deepening US-USSR Cold War tension, Russ called the police after he spotted Spira, who looked a bit like Soviet Premier leader Nikita Khrushchev.

After graduating from high school, I attended the Berkeley campus of the University of California from 1961 to 1965 and continued my education at CRDS in upstate New York. Whenever I returned home, I visited Russ, who lived with his infirmity for perhaps two decades. I was saddened when I learned he had died.

In 2011, Nancy and I attended the fiftieth anniversary of my Las Lomas graduation. We drove by Russ' home. While the creeks were largely invisible, and walnut groves had been reduced to a few trees, the hills were resplendent with wild golden poppies, the official state flower. These reminded me of my friend Russ who had been an inspiration in my life abundant.

12

Early Education

I BEGAN GRAMMAR SCHOOL in San Francisco's Sunset District. Around 1952 we moved to Walnut Creek where I attended Parkmead Elementary School. Mr. Rose taught geography. In an assignment for him, I drew a map of Africa. I located the capital of each country and included news clippings, photos from *National Geographic*, and stamps from my collection begun when our family received letters from relatives scattered throughout North and South America, Australia, Cameroon, and Israel.[1]

---

1. On visits to Israel, I have connected with several relatives including Ariel Tushinsky, related to aunt Olga Burstein, has performed as cellist with *The Jerusalem Trio*. I helped organize concerts for the group in Melbourne, Australia and Memphis, Tennessee. Other correspondents included Vitaly Kamoff, who was related to grandmother Vera Dovjenko. Vitaly left Russia and worked on a ship to earn money to help the family move to North America. During World War I, he was a crew member transporting timber to Europe from Cameroon, a German colony. After Britain and France gained control of the colony, Vitaly was arrested as a spy and remained in the country the rest of his life. On several occasions, Nancy and I visited with him in Douala. Irene Ehrenford, my Godmother, was also a relative of Vera Dovjenko. In 1961, when I graduated from high school, Irene and her husband Frank gifted me with a copy of *The Complete Poetical Works of James Whitcomb Riley* inscribed, "To dear Ricky, Irene and Frank, 1961." I last saw them when studying at the University of Chicago.

Early Education

I attended Las Lomas High School From 1957 to 1961. I did well scholastically from the start. My senior class entry in the 1960–1961 yearbook *El Caballero* read,

> "Deckar"; great zot!"; conservative; enjoys sports and traveling; hates Commies, especially Nikita [Khrushchev]; A. F. S., J. S. A., French club President, House of Rep. Palladians, and Knights of the Golden Key; bound for college.

My youthful conservativism grew out of the flight of my parents and other relatives from the "old country." As indicated in the year book entry, I hated "commies," especially Communist Russian leader Nikita Khrushchev. Events like the Bay of Pigs invasion of Cuba, Cuban missile crisis, and construction of the Berlin Wall engendered fear that so-called "cold war" between the US and former USSR would expand into nuclear war. I regarded as crazy the notion that we could survive a nuclear attack. MAD, "mutually assured destruction," characterized the US and USSR defense strategy.

Throughout high school, I was active in several organizations. American Field Service (A. F. S.) began by offering ambulance services to France during World War I. After the war, it morphed into a French interest group. Over the years it has evolved as a foreign exchange program. According to its most recent statistics, in 2023, A. F. S. exchange programs provided transformative, immersive experiences for close to eight thousand high school students, connecting them with host families and communities in over ninety countries. Since its founding, over five hundred thousand young people have participated in A. F. S. exchanges.

Another student-led organization I joined was Junior Statesmen of America (J. S. A.). For over eighty-five years, J. S. A. has trained young leaders to engage with civic issues. According to its website,

> Junior Statesmen of America prepares a diverse community of high school students to participate effectively in our democracy. We offer hands-on civic programs designed to activate the talents of young people, instill

values of respect and understanding, and inspire them to be a new generation of American leaders.

Throughout my Las Lomas years, I attended several J. S. A. events. In one case, around 1960, I was part of a delegation that visited Sacramento. We stayed at the Senator Hotel, now an office complex. While we waited in the lobby to check in, KCRA Channel 3 asked our group to go outside and then re-enter the state capitol building for a news clip. During the debate that ensued, someone made a point with which I did not agree. After I spoke, the first debater responded, "Sir you have water on the brain!" I don't recall my rejoinder.

Affiliating with national bodies like A. F. S. and J. S. A. sparked interest in wider politics. I was not yet eligible to vote in the 1960 election but, after John Fitzgerald Kennedy became president, I supported several initiatives of his administration, notably creation of the Peace Corps, the Alliance for Progress, and an agreement with Soviet leader Nikita Khrushchev that averted nuclear war over Cuba.

Las Lomas lacked diversity in the student body. Rick Scott was the sole African-American. Hideko Tani, a foreign exchange student from Japan during my last year, was the sole Asian American. Wernfried (Werni) Koeffler, another exchange student, came from Austria. Many years later, I served in the US diplomatic corps. In 1968, I sent Werni a Christmas letter from Cameroon. Werni replied that he had joined Austria's foreign service and expressed hope that "we might meet at some crazy place in this world."

I took four years of high school French. On one occasion, the French club went to San Francisco to see a French-themed film, *Gigi*, which in 1958 won several Academy Awards including Best Motion Picture. Our class ate at a French restaurant. I ordered roast duck. When I cut into it, the duck—slippery with a honey-balsamic glaze—landed on the lap of my teacher, Mademoiselle Johnson.

A number of students wrote yearbook entries in French. Some commented on my getting "A's." Membership in Palladians, an honor society, was based on grades. If we remained a member

Early Education

for enough semesters, we received at graduation a little pin in the shape of an oil lamp.

A photo of me with the tennis team accompanied my senior *El Caballero* entry. Until my fourth year, I had not been very active in sports, in part due to my mother's false claim that I suffered from asthma. As I needed a sport to graduate, she relented and let me participate on one team. I chose tennis, in part because the team needed another player for inter-school competition. I continued to play until my fifties when, experiencing back spasms, my family doctor advised that I find an alternative sport, which I did by taking up swimming, cycling, and curling years later.

During our senior year, Janet Fisher, Jane Irving, Don Jensen, Dave Zimmerman, and I were allowed to receive credit for courses taken at Diablo Valley College. Gaining post secondary school experience, I received a "B" grade in an introduction to humanities.

Three hundred and forty graduated in 1961. As salutatorian, I spoke. I have appended my address as an example of my early writing and public speaking.

Don Jensen, one my closest friends in those years, was class valedictorian. Among our favorite activities together, we hiked and camped along the John Muir Trail that extends over two hundred miles from Yosemite and other national parks to the Lake Tahoe area.

In 1964, along with Alan Smith, we hiked a week from Piute Pass through the Evolution Valley. I have a copy of our seven-day menu. By email dated November 1, 2022, Alan recalled this and other camping trips including one in 1961 when we went up highway 88 and camped at Silver Lake. Another year we climbed Mt. Dana next to Tioga Pass in Upper Yosemite Valley.

After attending Harvard for three years, Don graduated with a B.A. from Fresno State. In 1970, he received a Ph.D. in the field of mathematical logic from the University of Southern California. He taught two years at the University of Waterloo, Ontario, then at the University of Aberdeen, Scotland. Don also had a distinguished climbing career. Las Lomas classmate Pete Havens sent me copies of *Harvard Mountaineering* articles, featuring our hikes along the John

Muir Trail that extends along the Sierra Nevada mountain range, through Yosemite, Kings Canyon, and Sequoia National Parks.

In my high school freshman yearbook, *El Caballero*, Don thanked me for a ticket to a San Francisco Giants-Cincinnati Reds baseball game. He noted, "Some day I will convince you to be a Giants fan, like all good boys should. I hope to have lots of good pack trips with you this summer. Good luck again." Earlier I had been a Boston Red Sox fan due to its pillar player, Ted Williams, one of the greatest hitters in baseball history and the last player to hit over .400 in a season. Later, I did become a Giants fan, as well as an enthusiast for other Bay Area teams including the San Francisco 49ers (football), Golden State Warriors (basketball), and Oakland Athletics (baseball).

In the 1958–1959 edition, Don commented, "You're a terrific fellow with brains galore. You'll make a miraculous attorney—everybody will be guilty." He suggested that, if I wanted to learn German, his brother Lynn was in Germany and could help. He added, "will see you lots. Have fun in Seattle." This comment reflected that I spent part of the summer break with my grandparents Tommy and Margaret Kroviakoff.

Tragically in November 1973, Don died in a cycling accident in Aberdeen, Scotland where he was a visiting lecturer in mathematics. His brother Lynn, also a good scholar, died around the same time, as did their parents.

Another memory from my high school years was my first employment. I had several part-time jobs. At various times, I picked walnuts in season and repaired packing crates. Also, I substituted for my friend Alan Smith who had a job cleaning a lawyer's office.

During my early years, I established a life path that included commitment to academic success, interest in government, close friendships, and enjoyment of a variety of the arts and recreation. I have been forever grateful for having had such abundance and diversity of experience throughout my life.

13

University of California, Berkeley

I MAJORED IN POLITICAL science and minored in history at the Berkeley campus of the University of California from 1961 to 1965, years of great political and social unrest locally and worldwide. These upheavals affected significant my intellectual growth. I gained a solid liberal arts education. I began critically to evaluate what was happening in US society and to shift from a more conservative political orientation to a more progressive one.

My first academic advisor was Eugene Burdick, co-author with William Lederer of *The Ugly American* (1958). The book and the 1963 film based on it, which starred Marlon Brando as US ambassador Harrison MacWhite, inspired thoughts of a career either with the US Department of State, or in international law. The book and film also led me to be uncomfortable with the extent to which consumerism in the US and other highly developed nations depended on production of weapons and technologies of mass destruction.

However, the main impact of reading the book was in fueling my growing pacifism and desire to offer an alternative to existing priorities of US international engagement along lines described in the "factual epilogue" of *The Ugly American*,

We do not need the horde of 1,500,000 Americans—mostly amateurs—who are now working for the United States overseas. What we need is a small force of well-trained, well-chosen, hard-working, and dedicated professionals. They must be willing to risk their comforts and—in some lands—their health. They must go equipped to apply a positive policy promulgated by a clear-thinking government. They must speak the language of the land of their assignment, and they must be more expert in its problems than are the natives....

We have been offering the Asian nations the wrong kind of help. We have so lost sight of our own past that we are trying to sell guns and money alone, instead of remembering that it was the quest for the dignity of freedom that was responsible for our own way of life.

All over Asia we have found that the basic American ethic is revered and honored and imitated when possible. We must, while helping Asia toward self-sufficiency, show by example that America is still the America of freedom and hope and knowledge of law. If we succeed, we cannot lose the struggle.[1]

In my fourth year at Berkeley, I registered for a course with Dr. Burdick. Unfortunately, he fell ill before I could take his course. He died around the time of my graduation. Other professors contributed to my thinking about professional diplomatic service. In a course with Henry F. May, I surveyed the history of US foreign policy. Dr. May served at Berkeley from 1952 until 1980 and was department chair during the Free Speech Movement, the student protest that took place on our campus during the Fall 1964 term. In another course, I studied European diplomacy with Raymond J. Sontag, who taught at Berkeley from 1941 until he retired. Both professors wrote letters on my behalf when I applied for the US foreign service. Other courses contributed to my understanding of the Cold War.

During my Berkeley studies, I explored family roots. In a paper for a course on politics in the Soviet Union, I investigated whether Communism had enabled Russia to find practical

1. Burdick, *Ugly American*, 239–40.

solutions for contemporary problems. In a paper on the spirit of freedom in contemporary Russian thought," I reviewed three books: Mikhail Sholokhov, *Harvest on the Don* (1935), Arthur Koestler, *Darkness at Noon* (1940), and Boris Pasternack *Doctor Zhivago* (1958). I concluded as follows,

> Two ideas are brought into one pervading theme: the tragedy of the Bolshevik revolution is embodied in the repressive upheaval against which only spiritual opposition survives. The tragic events described in these three novels are consequential to a social revolution that attempted to destroy the spirit of a people, their will to live. Sholokhov, Koestler, and Pasternack express this yearning for true freedom. . . . Read together, we can grasp the violent effects of the 1917 Bolshevik *coup d'état* upon the masses of the now Communist Russia.

In a course on folklore, I collected examples of *blason populaire*, a genre that makes use of stereotypes (usually, but not always negative) of a particular group. Grandmother Vera Dovjenko mentioned the word "chalgon," by which she meant Siberians. She shared with me that the term literally means "thief" and is used as an insult. By inference, the person was assumed to be a criminal. In my project report, I observed, "In old Russia, criminals and revolutionaries were sent to Siberia. Mrs. Dovjenko is a refugee who came to the US from Siberia."

My first year, I lived at Barrington Hall, a cooperative where I worked in the kitchen. I shared a suite with two students who were too free-wheeling for me. Years later I received a letter from one of them, who wrote to apologize for his alcohol and drug abuse that had contributed to his failing and leaving the university, and to my decision to move elsewhere.

During my remaining three years at Berkeley, I lived at a Christian fraternity, Alpha Gamma Omega (AGO).[2] I shared a

---

2. Alpha is the first letter in the Greek alphabet. Omega is the last letter of the Greek alphabet. Gamma is the third letter and in this context refers to Jesus, so identified in Revelation 1:8; 21:6; and 22:13. Founded in 1938, AGO has chapters at several universities around the US.

suite with Eric Nelson. We were members of Valley Baptist Church. Some weekends, Eric and I commuted home with Eric's sister Carol Nelson [Eklund]. Carol drove. When we came to a stop, Eric and I sometime jumped out and circled the car.³ Notwithstanding, or because of such antics, we became lifelong friends.

With my fraternity brothers, I played intermural sports including basketball, tennis, and running. I did several ten-kilometer races until back spasms led my family doctor to recommend that I take up other games. I tried golf, for which I received a sports credit needed to graduate. However, despite occasional forays on various links, I never became proficient in the sport.

I spent two years in the required Reserve Officers Training Corps program. I learned to spit polish my shoes and to march in uniform in gatherings around the west coast as did a beloved cousin Nick Romanzov, whose military service overlapped with mine.⁴

Later in my Berkeley years, I moved in the direction of pacifism and commitment to peace and justice work. Crucial was my having attended a talk about the Fellowship of Reconciliation (FOR), founded on the eve of World War I. Among delegates at a peace conference trying to prevent war, Fredrich Siegmund-Schultze, chaplain to the German Kaiser and Henry Hodgkin, an English Quaker, shook hands and joined a hundred and thirty delegates in forming a significant interfaith peace organization with the following statement of mission: "Love, as revealed and

---

3. This is known as Chinese fire drill. A real Chinese fire drill occurred in Chico, California in 1881 at the peak of anti-Chinese hysteria in the state. End of a street were blocked, houses set on fire, and Chinese residents fleeing from burning buildings were shot.

4. Born February 8, 1943, Nick and I often celebrated our common birth date together. A relative of my maternal grandfather, Nick and I regarded each other as cousins. After serving in the US military, Nick received financial aid from Veterans Affairs, trained as an engineer and then worked for the US Corps of Army Engineers. Nick's wife Jeannette was of Mexican descent. Nick was outraged when he was assigned to work on plans for a canal or security wall along the US/Mexico border. Grieving Jeannette's death of cancer, Nick died January 29, 1994). Nick appeared briefly in the film *The Russians Are Coming! The Russians Are Coming!* (1966).

interpreted in the life and death of Jesus Christ, involves more than we have yet seen, that it is the only power by which evil can be overcome, and the only sufficient basis of human society."[5]

Impressed by FOR's advocacy against all wars, I signed its statement of purpose and joined its campaigns against required military training and stocking bomb shelters. I participated for the first time in civil disobedience, a protest against growing US involvement in Vietnam, was arrested, and quickly released without charges.

As an FOR member, I received a copy of *Fellowship*, through which I learned about the Trappist monk Thomas Merton. I read some of his essays including "The Root of War is Fear" and "The Shelter Ethic" in *The Catholic Worker*. Such writing led the US Catholic hierarchy briefly to advise Catholics not to read Merton until September 24, 2015, when Pope Francis addressed a joint session of US Congress. In his talk, he honored the memory of four Americans: Abraham Lincoln, Martin Luther King, Jr., Dorothy Day, and Thomas Merton, who he described as a "source of spiritual inspiration and a guide for many people.... Merton was above all a man of prayer, a thinker who challenged the certitudes of his time and opened new horizons for souls and for the Church. He was also a man of dialogue, a promoter of peace between peoples and religions."[6]

I served two years in student government, first as a Junior class officer and then as "Representative-at-Large" on the Associated Students of the University of California (ASUC) Senate. In my campaign for the latter office, I focused on efforts to increase student services and professional outcomes. After I won the election, I implemented some of these proposals on campus.

In terms of wider politics, during the Spring of 1964, New York Governor Nelson A. Rockefeller came to campus while campaigning for the Republican nomination for the upcoming presidential campaign. By chance, I shook hands on three places during

---

5. Dekar, *Creating the Beloved Community*, 32; Dekar, *Dangerous People*, 4; Dekar, "Forging Bonds and Obligations," 108.

6. Pope Francis, *Merton Annual*, 21.

his campus visit. The first time was at the intersection of Bancroft and Telegraph Avenues, a main campus entry. I was distributing anti-war leaflets at a table. As Rockefeller arrived, the governor shook hands with me and others. Later, he came by Ludwig's Fountain, named after a dog who used to bathe in it, where I was eating my lunch. We again shook hands. He greeted me a third time as I entered the building where he had given a talk. I never mentioned that I supported President Lyndon Johnson's campaign for re-election.

My Berkeley years expanded my appreciation of and participation in the arts. I attended lectures and concerts at the Greek Theatre, an eight thousand, five hundred-seat open-air amphitheater overlooking the Bay Area. I still play vinyl records that I purchased after attending concerts by such performers as Joan Baez, Glen Yarborough, and Peter, Paul, and Mary. I developed a life-long interest in cinema, especially foreign language films that I saw at a nearby cinema where I had free admission in exchange for ushering.

As graduation approached, I considered applying to the Peace Corps or law school. Neither option materialized. I was named to the Senior Hall of Fame and Order of the Golden Bear, an honor society committed to serving the University of California. My yearbook entry reads:

> Paul Dekar has held many student offices. Elected Rep-at-Large to the ASUC Senate, and Senate class Yell Leader, Paul has also been Chairman of Operations Committee, and a member of Class Officers Board, Gavel and Quill, and Order of the Golden Bear. An Honors at entrance student with three years of University Scholarships, Paul was President of his fraternity, Alpha Gamma Omega. His future plans include using his Political Science major and History-French minor in both seminary studies and local politics.[7]

Reflecting on my University of California years, I graduated well prepared academically and professionally, first as a diplomat,

---

7. *Blue and Gold*, 85.

University of California, Berkeley

then in Christian ministry and ultimately in academic life. As well, my four years at Berkeley fueled idealism succinctly described by President Kennedy in his 1961 inaugural address when he stated that we should not ask what our country can do for us, but what one can do for one's country. As well, outgoing Dwight David Eisenhower's warning in his final speech as president about the military industrial complex heightened my growing pacifist convictions

As for interest in local politics, I considered running for political office in the early 1980s. An initial foray into raising money to seek nomination for an upcoming provincial election made me uncomfortable. I was relieved when a friend, Richard Allen, distinguished historian and colleague at McMaster University, ran successfully for the open seat.

Finally, my studies contributed to my moving away from the more conservative perspective I had imbibed in my earlier years as the son of immigrant parents. By the end of my university studies, I had adopted the more progressive and global outlook that has subsequently characterized my life abundant.

14

Free Speech Movement

THE FREE SPEECH MOVEMENT (FSM) dominated the Berkeley campus during the Fall 1964 term. Until then, the university administration had allowed student groups to raise funds only for Democratic and Republican Party clubs. When students who had traveled with the Freedom Riders and worked to register African-American voters in Mississippi began raising funds for such causes, the administration sought to bar such activity. Ignoring such restrictions, student activists continued to set up information tables on campus and to solicit donations for off-campus organizations connected to the wider civil rights movement.

When on September 14, 1964, the administration banned such activity, students were outraged. There had been no input by students regarding the new regulations that specifically forbade fundraising, membership recruitment, and political speeches on campus property. Along with the wider FSM movement, I considered a major role of universities to be promotion of active citizenship. I deemed the new regulations as a violation of freedom of speech, guaranteed by the US Constitution, specifically the First Amendment, which protects the freedom of speech, religion, and the press as well as the right of people peaceably to assemble and to petition the Government for a redress of grievances. The amendment was adopted in 1791 along with nine other amendments that make up the Bill of Rights, a document that incorporated fundamental civil liberties along lines of the English Magna Carta (1215) and various colonial charters like those of Rhode Island or Pennsylvania. These reflected the legacies of Roger Williams, William Penn, and other political theorists that I read in my political science courses.

Protesting the new rules, students formed a "United Front" of some twenty organizations that advocated restoration of the tables and rejected limited the free speech of students. Over the next two weeks, the United Front held rallies. On October 1, 1964, Mario Savio, United Front leader and onetime graduate student, refused to show his identification to the campus police. Along with several others, Savio was arrested. In response, students surrounded the police car in which he was to be transported. Such civil disobedience was central to the movement.

On December 4, 1964, police cordoned off Sproul Hall and arrested close to eight hundred students. Most were quickly released. A month later, the university brought charges against the students who responded by organizing a sit-in. This led to an even larger protest that all but shut down the university. As the movement gained international attention, a variety of speakers and performers came. Joan Baez sang a benefit concert for the FSM defence fund.

In one rally, I heard Mario Savio, acknowledged FSM leader, summarize the movement's demands:

> Last summer I went to Mississippi to join the struggle there for civil rights. This fall I am engaged in another phase of the same struggle, this time in Berkeley. The two battlefields may seem quite different to some observers, but this is not the case. The same rights are at stake in both places—the right to participate as citizens in a democratic society and their right to due process of law. We are asking that our actions be judged by committees of our peers. We are asking that regulations ought to be considered as arrived at legitimately only from a consensus of the governed.[1]

---

1. Warshaw, *Trouble in Berkely*, 27.

By January 3, 1965, a new acting chancellor, Martin Meyerson established new, provisional rules for political activity on the Berkeley campus. These designated the Sproul Hall steps as an open discussion area during certain hours of the day and permitted information tables. Over the period of several months, according to Mario Savio,

> ... the focus of our attention shifted from our deep concern with the victimization of others to outrage at the injustices done to ourselves. These injustices we came to perceive more and more clearly with each new attack upon us by the university bureaucracy as we sought to secure our own rights to political advocacy. The political consciousness of the Berkeley community has been quickened by this fight. The Berkeley students now demand what hopefully the rest of an oppressed white middle class will some day demand: freedom for all Americans, not just for Negroes![2]

The FSM radicalized me. I had already demonstrated against required reserve officer training, preparations for nuclear war and growing US involvement in Vietnam. While not among the activists arrested during the FSM, I learned strategies of nonviolent resistance adapted to other controversies at Berkeley. As well, during my two years in student government, I was able to mediate in several conflicts and thereby to support needed changes on campus and in wider society.

As an FSM ally, I developed awareness of my right and obligation to protest injustice. In helping make the Berkeley campus freer, more open, and more pluralistic, my participation in such extra-curricular activities contributed as much to my education as did any class taught by the university's distinguished faculty. Increasingly engaged in human rights, peace, and social justice movements, I identified with the "waves of protest" influencing social life in the US and beyond during the nineteen sixties.[3]

---

2. Draper, *Berkeley: The New Student Revolt*, 6.
3. Title of a book edited by Freeman and Johnson.

15

1962 APBA Season

Over several years, I played three or four baseball seasons through APBA, a baseball simulation game with dice, a set of player cards for every major-league team for a season and roughly ten by twelve-inch charts for results in situations such as bases empty, bases loaded, rare plays, or base stealing. Although I could play alone, I enjoyed sharing the game with my brother George. After each World Series, we ordered the new cards, picked our favorite teams, and played the entire season. Our results usually replicated those of the actual season and World Series.

During the 1962 major league season, George and I attended several games of our favorite team, the San Francisco Giants. This culminated their fifth year in San Francisco since their move from New York and their third at Candlestick Park, the love-it or hate-it stadium where for years the Giants played in a wind-swept area to the south of the city.

Did I mention wind-swept? Like when Giants relief pitcher Stu Miller got blown off the mound during the 1961 All-Star Game. The umpire charged him with a balk, and it was recorded as a blown save.

The 1962 World Series pitted the National League champion San Francisco Giants, and the American League champion New York Yankees. The Yankees won the series in seven games. However

Life Abundant

much George and I wanted to attend one of the World Series games, we had to content ourselves with re-playing the season and with APBA cards due to the cost of tickets for post-season games.

I recall a story from the '62 World Series. A fan had travelled some distance to see the great centerfielders, Willie Mays and Mickey Mantle. Watching a few games from centerfield, the fan called out, "Hey Mantle, I can't decide who is worse between you and Mays." Pausing a few seconds, after Mays made a brilliant catch, the fan added, "Mantle, you win!"

Apocryphal? Not really. Mantle contributed mightily to the Yankee's success that season. But in that World Series play, he hit a pathetic .120 over the seven games and drove in no runs.

But this did not factor in when George and I did the 1962 series with APBA cards. Playing the Yankees, George won a game in which Mantle hit a home run which he had not done in real time. Joking, Geoge challenged my assertion that Mays was the greatest, especially for his fielding prowess. Playing the Yankees APBA cards at the end of the season, George emerged victorious in the 1962 World Series.

As George declined into mental illness, I visited with him as often as I could. If in season, I accompanied George to watch the Oakland As play at a coliseum, a half hour away from Rheem Valley, where he lived until our mother could no longer care for him. We also played the 1972, 1973 and 1974 ABPA seasons during which the Oakland A's won three World Series with future Hall-of-Famers Rollie Fingers, Catfish Hunter, and Reggie Jackson. While I have not continued to play ABPA, my elder son Nathaniel plays a modified version with his friends, GIMBA—the Garth Iorg Memorial Baseball Association, named after a former Blue Jays infielder.[1]

In 1976, Nancy, Nathaniel and I moved to Hamilton, Ontario. I sometimes joked that I accepted a teaching position at

---

1. During my Memphis years, I attended games of the Memphis Chicks in the Southern League. After retiring from active baseball, Garth Iorg was coaching a team playing against the Chicks. I called out to him, and told him about GIMBA. Pleased he autographed a ball team for me to pass on to Nathaniel.

McMaster University only after American League expansion included the Toronto Blue Jays. Ever since, we have attended many Blue Jays games.

Early during our Hamilton years, Nancy and I could buy $4 seats for $2 at Dominion Grocery. By attending an afternoon game at Exhibition Stadium in late August through and including Labor Day, we could enter, gratis, the Canadian National Exhibition grounds after the game.

In 1989, a new stadium replaced Exhibition Stadium as home of the Blue Jays. With a retractable roof stadium, this stadium serves as an all-weather facility. Given the price my granddaughter Abbey has paid to treat me, Nancy, and her dad to a couple recent Blue Jays games, I find it difficult to recall we once could get $2 tickets. While I no longer play fantasy baseball, I have taken great pleasure watching my sons and their children play baseball and other sports, a major component of my life abundant.

16

Yellowstone National Park, 1962 and 2023

I TWICE WORKED WITH Christian Ministries in the National Parks, an ecumenical program of the National Council of the Churches of Christ in the US. The program's purpose was, and remains to offer students interested in a career in Christian ministry a chance to gain experience in a context the inspires awe in the miracle of creation.

In 1962, I was assigned to Yellowstone National Park in Wyoming. I found a ride to Salt Lake City after which I hitchhiked to the park, something I can not now imagine having done. Six days a week from June 9 to September 6, I worked as a fountain clerk at the Canyon Village General Store, near the Old Faithful geyser. Saturday evenings, I distributed throughout the campgrounds an invitation to worship the next morning.

Each Sunday, I led worship, taught classes and facilitated special events like presenting Handel's *Messiah*. The "Yellowstone choir" performed it as part of a celebration of "Christmas in the park." In a letter to my family, kept in a scrapbook from that experience, I explained that I worked hard but found organizing Sunday School difficult as many "brats" attended.

In August, low wages—$85 per month plus room and board—and low morale led nearly a hundred permanent staff to

Yellowstone National Park, 1962 and 2023

strike. *The Billings [Montana] Gazette* reported a successful outcome for the strikers.

I enjoyed fishing, horse back riding and bird watching on my days off. A few osprey nests were usually visible near the Canyon Village. While I did not swim in the glacier-fed waters of the Yellowstone River, I was deeply moved by the beautiful grand canyon it had carved out of the mountains. In my scrapbook, I observed, "We can never forget whose creation this mighty park is. Now I know why I believe!"

In 1966, I did a second stint with the program in Lassen National Park in Northern California. I served as a grocery clerk and organized Sunday worship. On my days off, I hiked through the area. This included an ascent of Mount Lassen, which was still an active volcano, or reading books including Rachel Carson's *Silent Spring*, which heightened my commitment to earth care.

More recently, in 2023, I visited a small area in the northern part of Yellowstone National Park along with Nancy and several of our traveling group of Memphis friends. On a couple of days, we entered the northern parts of Yellowstone. In the Lamar Valley and along the Beartooth Trail, we saw wildlife for which the park is famous: birds, bison, black and grizzly bears, elk, pika, and pronghorn, but no wolves. We marveled at spectacular vistas of fields, mountains, waterfalls, and the Mammoth Hot Springs.

At one stop, I asked a ranger what has changed over his nearly sixty years growing up and working in the park. He observed that, unlike the past, most contemporary visitors live in highly urbanized communities. Many are indifferent towards nature, unaware that their actions are contributing to climate change. Many ignore warnings NOT to approach or feed the animals. Our brief conversation recalled the "haunting indifference of nature," a phrase of Jill Lapore who wrote an article "The Bear in Your Back Yard," (*New Yorker*, July 17, 2023).

While I fear the adverse consequences of the haunting indifference towards nature on the part of some visitors, I trust that most enjoy such wilderness places as Yellowstone, as I have. Capitalizing on the popularity of Lewis Carroll's *Alice's Adventures in*

Wonderland, early promoters of Yellowstone nicknamed the park "Wonderland." So it remains, as does our need to redouble efforts to care for our endangered world. Such travel, educational and professional experience were essential to my growth and life abundant. May it be so for others.

17

Camp Counselor

DURING THE SUMMER OF 1963, I worked at Mount Herman. It was a church sponsored camp in rural Santa Cruz County a few miles from Monterey. Founded in 1906, Mount Herman was the first Christian Camp west of the Mississippi River. Along with an additional center, Mount Hermon continues to fulfill the vision of its founders to share the Gospel of Jesus as Lord and Savior, to teach the *Bible* and to serve the church worldwide.

During orientation, I learned how to share my faith with campers using "four spiritual laws." These were intended to help people understand their spiritual circumstances and to come to a relationship with God. The four principles were the following:

- God loves us and has a wonderful plan for us.
- Sin separates us from God.
- Jesus is the only way to know God's love and plan.
- We must individually receive Jesus as our Savior.

For several months after that Summer, I corresponded with campers who shared that their experience had been life-changing. For myself, in addition to benefiting my educational and spiritual development, I enjoyed walking through the woods and experiencing the natural beauty of the surrounding area. This contributed to a sense of abundance of life.

My family also loved the area and visited several times. We sometimes went to what is now the Big Basin Redwoods State Park. Established in 1902, it is California's oldest state park and is still home to the largest continuous stand of coast redwoods south of San Francisco. Many are over a thousand years old. The park also offers spectacular views of the Pacific Ocean, many babbling brooks and a fascinating cultural history.

In 2011, Nancy and I traveled to California for my fiftieth anniversary high school class reunion. I wanted to introduce Nancy to key areas of my growing up. We visited the Redwoods State Park, drove along the 17-Mile Monterey Peninsula drive, much of which hugs the Pacific and ate at restaurant owned by the actor Clint Eastwood. Despite the experience of some visitors, we did not meet the actor.

As part of my sharing places crucial in my growing up, Nancy and I continued to Yosemite National Park where we spent several days in Yosemite Valley with such points of interest as El Capitan and Mirror Lake, followed by a few additional days in the High Sierras. Opportunities to work and play in such wonders of nature have been central to my life abundant.

18

Organizing for Change

DURING THE SUMMER OF 1964, I worked for the city of Berkeley as recreation director at a neighborhood park. I also participated in a North Oakland/Emeryville Summer Service Project that grew from the ministry of Faith Presbyterian Church where Lou Lucky, cook at my fraternity was a member. The congregation designed the project for university students interested in "meaningful service" during the Summer in a "predominantly Negro community."[1]

Saul D. Alinsky, a Chicago-based organizer inspired the project. Alinsky's Industrial Areas Foundation helped poor communities organize to press demands upon landlords, politicians, bankers and business leaders. Alinksy urged that activists organize locally, drawing on the experience of those involved directly, whatever the issue at hand may be. Alinsky imbued confidence that structural change was possible. Inspiring hope that activists could help build an alternative society different than that in the US, I came to resist militarism and consumerism.

---

1. Project Brochure. In my notebook, I used language of the day, hence Negro, not African American. The black power movement had not yet emerged. I read recommended books such as Charles E. Silberman, *Crisis in Black and White* and James Baldwin, *A Fire Next Time*. Given lack of African Americans in my early years, these books and the project were my first deep exposure to black-white issues.

Life Abundant

Since Alinsky's death in 1972, his organization has continued to help ordinary citizens share in the public arena with the goal of improving conditions in their neighbourhoods and cities. Especially important for me, Alinksy concluded his book *Rules for Radicals* as follows,

> The great American dream that reached out to the stars has been lost to the stripes. We have forgotten where we came from, we don't know where we are, and we fear where we may be going. Afraid, we turn from the glorious adventure of the pursuit of happiness to a pursuit of an illusionary security in an ordered, stratified, striped society. Our way of life is symbolized to the world by the stripes of military force. At home we have made a mockery of being our brother's keeper by being his jail keeper. When American can no longer see the stars, the times are tragic. We must believe that it is the darkness before the dawn of a beautiful new world; we will see it when we believe it.[2]

Drawing on this resource, I helped organize street recreation and register voters for the 1964 election. On occasion, I attended Faith Presbyterian Church for worship or special sessions. I became outraged over the problems faced by African-Americans and by the extent to which the US government could finance the military to the detriment of its ability to address poverty or other social needs. I grew pessimistic due to lack of progress in addressing injustice and racism. In my journal, I noted the need for "massive change and massive compensation," an issue currently being addressed by calls—and opposition to such calls—in the US to provide African-Americans reparations and for anti-discrimination policies that remove barriers to economic justice.

In 1977, after Nancy, Nathaniel, and I had settled in Hamilton, Ontario, I participated in two programs of a similar neighborhood organization, the Locke Street Business Improvement Area Association. One was a food cooperative through which Nancy and I did a regular shift serving customers. Another spin-off, the

---

2. Alinsky, *Rules for Radicals*, 196.

Kirkendall Recreation Association (KRA), provided t-ball, softball, and soccer opportunities for girls and boys of primary school age. As a coach and, for several years, as director of the program, I emphasized such principles as collegiality, skill-development, and learning from their experience.

I sought to create a safe and supportive environment in which young people could have fun and grow. I encouraged participants to play several positions. I recruited coaches who shared my philosophy, and when possible, to co-coach. These measures provided flexibility as Summer schedules often made it difficult to field a full team due to varied family commitments. Also, to emphasize skill development, we did not keep score or standings.

Several parents began to complain that a coach pushed kids to win at any cost and berated them if they made mistakes. Responding to the parents, I observed the coach in action and confirmed why folks were upset. I spoke with the coach. When he continued his negative coaching, I had to dismiss him.

Years later, the coach in question approached and thanked me. He explained that, at the time, his marriage was falling apart, that he was having trouble at work, and that he inadvertently was taking out his frustrations on the kids. By firing him, I had jolted him to greater self consciousness and contributed to his personal healing. His marriage survived. He retooled and found new employment. In a sense, he had recovered from a cultural win-at-any-cost addiction.

When I passed the mantle of KRA leadership to my successor, parents gave me a "Coach of the Year" statue. Over the years, I met some of the coaches and youth in other circumstances. They thanked me for having recognized their strengths, potential and, sometimes, weaknesses. On a couple occasions, they asked me to officiate at weddings or other life-passage events.

Through community organizing, I believe I fostered involvement in sports in a less competitive manner than characteristic of some programmes of the day and in local organizing that, in the case of the Locke Street organization has facilitated a significant upgrade of the area. Thus resisting cultural priorities like material

LIFE ABUNDANT

gain or winning, I have continued to stress self-awareness and personal growth on the part of young people I have mentored as well as an approach to living that has imparts a great sense of satisfaction in my life abundant.

19

Operation Crossroads Africa, Chad

DURING THE 1964–1965 ACADEMIC year I was waiting at a bus stop to return home from Berkeley for the weekend when I noticed a poster advertising Summer international exchanges through Operation Crossroads Africa (OCA). Presbyterian clergyperson James Herman Robinson founded this non-profit, non-governmental organization in 1958. Forerunner of the US Peace Corps, OCA and its Canadian counterpart annually sent three hundred and fifty young persons to Africa.

In 1965, I joined a delegation to Fort Lamy, Chad. The city, renamed N'Djamena in 1973, is located on the country's southwestern border with Cameroon. Fort Lamy was and is the capital and largest city of the country. At the time, it had a population of just over a hundred thousand. The following draws from my trip diary.

June 13, 1965, a few days before orientation, I flew to New York City. A niece of a Berkeley friend offered hospitality. We visited the Statue of Liberty, Central Park, Stock Exchange, United Nations and Metropolitan Museum of Art about which I journaled, "the most fabulous collection I have ever seen." Picasso's *Guernica*, painted in reaction to the devastation of the Basque town during the Spanish Civil War, especially moved me.

I took a bus to Boston. Another host facilitated my touring the "Freedom Trail," with the USS Constitution (Old Ironsides), a frigate of the US Navy and, at the time, the oldest ship afloat. I enjoyed a drive to Cape Cod past Hyannis Port, home of the Kennedy family that has long been prominent in US politics. Among other places visited, Waldon Pond was disappointing due to commercialization. I then continued to Rutgers University in New Jersey for orientation after which several Crossroader groups flew on Air France to Lagos, Nigeria.

There, I was overwhelmed by the sprawling city, already the largest in Africa, with its enormous contrasts of poverty and wealth and myriad ethnic groups with varying dress, body markings, and languages. A US embassy official introduced the countries where we would work. We learned of a possible war in the eastern part of Nigeria.[1] Already aware of culture shock, we continued to Ibadan, Nigeria's third-largest city by population after Lagos and Kano in the North. We continued through Nigeria by train, bus, and truck. We crossed the Chari River into Chad by pirogue, a dugout canoe made from a log. We spotted hippos nearby.

Upon arriving in Fort Lamy, we met our Chadian counterparts and soon began construction of a primary school. We typically worked early in the morning. Dry heat precluded work during peak daytime hours. After lunch, I tended to nap, after which I was free and sometimes walked to a nearby market, read or played *boules* a French game similar to lawn bowling or *bocce*. The objective was to throw or roll heavy balls as closely as possible to a target. To improve my French-language skill, I read *L'Étranger* by Albert Camus.

In a letter to friends dated July 1, 1965 I wrote,

> The work is hard, and we are up at 6:30 (yes, even little ol' me), stopping at 12:30 because of the heat. We have nearly completed the foundations, but it is unlikely that we shall finish the building, as the work is slow. A laborer receives only 157 Central African Francs a day, little more than 80 cents. We live in the dorms of a nearby high school

---

1. In 1967, eastern Nigeria, inhabited predominantly by the Igbo ethnic group, declared independence. Biafra existed as an independent state until 1970. Working in Cameroon with the US Department of State between 1968–1970, I was able to assist Biafran refugees fleeing the civil war in Nigeria.

with several African students who are official guides and friends for the Summer. The afternoons are spent resting, writing, reading, and sharing ideas and experiences with our new friends, who are eager to learn of America. . . . There are so many experiences to share, such as getting to know US ambassador Brewster H. Morris, eating Arab food on a Muslim holiday, walking along the Chari River, watching a hippo, drinking palm wine in the villages nearby, and dancing the highlife. . . . The group calls me Reverend, or *le Pasteur* . . . playful kidding has opened up some deep and probing discussions. Sharing ideas with Moslem friends has been a real highpoint of my experience. . . . The conservative Protestant church is growing.

In a later diary entry, I noted that our progress impressed everybody. We worked with a dozen Chadians, including a daughter of the country's first head of state, François Tombalbaye. One morning, President Tombalbaye and members of his cabinet visited the worksite. We gave them Crossroads pins. The president asked how the US was dealing with desegregation, and about our experience in Chad. He provided a Chadian meal of couscous, a local grain served with goat meat and vegetables, followed by French (!) pastries.

In part through the assistance of Ambassador Morris, our delegation and Chadian counterparts had several opportunities to ferry along the Chari and Legogne rivers. We carefully avoided hippos! We also flew to the Chad-Sudan border. On July 10, I noted that we saw a Moslem wedding and dancers. A couple days later, we celebrated a national holiday, the birth of the Muslim prophet Mohammed.

As our Chad sojourn neared its end, our delegation debated where we might "vacation." I proposed that we to go to Lambarene, Gabon, to visit the hospital served by Albert Schweitzer, a childhood hero. I suspected Schweitzer did not have much longer to live. At the time, I was unaware of complexities in his legacy about which I learned later from missionary doctors serving in Cameroon near the Gabon border. Dr. Schweitzer died September 4, 1965.

Instead, we opted to visit Yaoundé, the capital of Cameroon, and Douala, the country's commercial center. We toured rain forest and enjoyed swimming at some beaches. We then flew to Fernando Po, now called Bioko Island. At the time, it had a relatively well-developed tourist industry. We stayed at a hotel overlooking the harbor and ocean and toured the island with its lush rain forest and prosperous cocoa and coffee plantations. While it was still a Spanish colony, preparations for independence along with the mainland area Rio Muni were under way. Now the Republic of Equatorial Guinea, it remains one of the poorest vestiges of Africa's colonial past.

Over the next few years, I kept in touch with some of our Chadian counterparts. In one case, I received a photo of the completed building accompanied, not surprisingly, by a scholarship request. I later learned that the school had been destroyed during the Chadian–Libyan War, a series of military campaigns between 1978 and 1987.

Although I did not plan this at the time, this entry into Africa prepared me for my posting, two years later, to Cameroon as a US diplomat. It also stimulated interest in African studies, a focus of my graduate work. I learned to appreciate new foods, music, especially the highlife, and caution, especially around drinking water. Finally, it provided satisfaction of contributing to efforts by Chadians to develop their education system.

In these ways, my Summer with OCA anticipated key aspects of my life abundant. Travel to forty countries has provided a rich experience in cultural, religious, and social diversity. Equally important, working on projects that have contributed to bettering the lives of others has enabled me to seek to ensure that every individual—indeed all creatures great and small, to borrow words of a popular television series—enjoys a life of abundance.

20

Seminary

As GRADUATION FROM UCB neared, I prepared to apply for law school. At the time, I shared a suite with Eric Nelson at AGO, where I lived three of my four Berkeley years. We were members of Valley Baptist Church. Learning of my intent to attend law school, Eric, his sister Carol, and their mother Mary alerted her brother, John Skoglund, of my plans. Dr. Skoglund taught preaching and worship at CRDS, a progressive theological school in Rochester, New York. Out of the blue, I received a full scholarship to CRDS provided by an upstate New York congregation.

Before accepting the grant, I did some research and was attracted by the academic legacy of the seminary. I learned that a key figure in the social gospel movement of the early twentieth century, Walter Rauschenbusch, had taught there and had inspired the Reverend Dr. Martin Luther King, Jr. As well, the seminary's professor of theology, William H. Hamilton, was at the center of the so-called "death of God" movement.

The phrase "death of God" drew from the writings of the nineteenth-century German philosopher Friedrich Nietzsche. In a chapter of a book co-authored with another theologian, Thomas J. J. Altizer, Dr. Hamilton explained the meaning of the phrase "death of God" as follows,

What does it mean to say that God is dead? Is this any more than a rather romantic way of pointing to the traditional difficulty of speaking about the holy God in human terms? Is it any more than a warning against all idols, all divinities fashioned out of human need, human ideologies? Does it perhaps not just mean that "existence is not an appropriate word to ascribe to God, that therefore he cannot be said to exist, and he is in that sense dead"? It surely means all this, and . . . more than the old protest against natural theology or metaphysics; more than the usual assurance that before the holy God all our language gets broken and diffracted into paradox. It is really that we do not know, do not adore, do not possess, do not believe in God. . . . God is dead. We are not talking about the absence of the experience of God, but about the experience of the absence of God.[1]

The death of God movement gained considerable attention through publication of a lecture series under the title *Varieties of Unbelief* by historian Martin E. Marty and an article in the April 8, 1966 edition of *Time Magazine* entitled "Is God Dead?" In part because of Dr. Hamilton's radical orientation, the area minister for the American Baptist Convention in the western US advised against my attending CRDS. He cautioned that few ABC churches would call me as pastor.

I was not deterred and looked forward to the opportunity of studying with Dr. Hamilton, who proved to be an inspiring teacher. I appreciated his first-year introductory course. Despite having little exposure to writings by female theologians, I was well grounded in writings by leading theologians including Dietrich Bonhoeffer, Reinhold Niebuhr, Paul Tillich, and Walter Rauschenbusch, a point I emphasized later when I applied for graduate school.

Arriving in Rochester in September 1965, I found a city immersed in civil rights strife.[2] These arose in part from procedures

1. Hamilton, *Radical Theology*, 26-28.
2. For background, article by R. D. G. Wadhwani in *The Historian* 60, No. 1 (Fall 1997): 59–75 and *Rochester. The Quest for Quality* by Blake McKelvey, who inscribed my copy, "To Paul R. Dekar with best wishes for his projected seminar on Rochester in the Rauschenbusch Era."

for getting jobs at two of the larger employers in the region, The Eastman Kodak Company, or Kodak, noted for products related to photography, and Xerox.

After race riots erupted in Rochester in 1964, organizers formed FIGHT—Freedom, Independence, God, Honor, Today—that successfully lobbied for better hiring practices and living conditions. In part because of the school's historical association with civil rights, these issues dominated conversation during my time at the seminary and eventually erupted in a major protest.

While I was not at the school at the time, on March 2, 1969, nineteen students entered the main academic building and locked and chained the doors in protest. The lockout was led by the black student caucus. The assassination in Memphis, Tennessee of the Reverend Dr. Martin Luther King, Junior on April 4, 1968 served as a catalyst. By the time the lockout ended, the school had committed to a black church studies program that was in place when I returned for my third year in the program.

As for other classes, I enjoyed the introductory preaching and worship course with John Skoglund. He introduced me to the concept of a lectionary, a three-year cycle with Gospel texts from Matthew, Mark, or Luke and passages from John incorporated at other times. Over the years, when asked to preach, I generally have used the lectionary texts of the day.

Prentiss L. Pemberton, or "Pem" was another CRDS faculty member who had a lasting impact on me. He taught social ethics and was a member of South Avenue Baptist Church where I did two years of required field work. Pem's mentoring solidified my growing opposition to US military engagement in Southeast Asia.

In retirement, Pem lived in Decatur, Georgia, where he joined Oakhurst Baptist Church. In 1984, I visited the congregation. Pem's pastor Nancy Sehested, wife of our executive director, Ken Sehested, took me to visit Pem at his care facility. She warned that he might not remember me. To her surprise, and my joy, he welcomed me and gave me a copy of his book, *Toward a Christian Economic Ethic* signed, "with love in Christ, Pem, January 14, 1984."

Christian history interested me and ultimately shaped my doctoral work and teaching. Charles Neilson taught early, medieval, and Reformation courses. Winthrop Hudson taught contemporary Christianity. His seminar on modern Catholicism included a unit on monasticism. With his encouragement, I visited for a few days Mount Savior Monastery near Elmyra, New York. I was impressed by the monks, who sought to live a simple, genuine and full monastic life according to the Scriptures and the *Rule of St. Benedict*.

Drawing on my experience in Chad, I made an initial foray into African studies, that became a major focus of my doctoral work. In addition to reading novels by African writers and books by Kenyan-born John Mbiti.

During my first two years at CRDS, I co-edited and contributed an occasional poem or article for the seminary newsletter, *Hilltop Views*. In a poem, entitled "Being of Age," I wrote:

> The world is charged with the action of God.
> Plei Me and Da Nang, immoral outposts of Hell,
> Flame out, recking and inflicting with pain. . . .
> Whither God, enter godliness, the world has awaited
> The death. For with death is thirst and resurrection.
> Without the myth we are free to spurn and to die,
> To strength and to action, not to choice and to taction
> A pact of commerce, taxes, tears, reminding
> In as much as to the least you have been, you are.

A key feature of my theological education was field work. I did two years under the mentorship of Gordon Kurtz at South Avenue Baptist Church. The church was a short walk from the seminary through beautiful Highland Park. In the Fall, the park's deciduous trees provided an array of color before the leaves fell off. In the Spring, the park's lilac dell signaled the end of Winter. During my first experience of snowfall, I wondered if conditions were such that I called the Kurtz' to ask if services had been cancelled before setting off to walk through Highland Park to the church.

During the 1970–1971 academic year, my third at CRDS, I was assigned to a Catholic parish where I helped the congregation form a church council. I recall conversations with the priest on the challenges of implementing reforms of the Second Vatican Council.

That year I also part-time employment with the chaplaincy office of the University of Rochester. My role on the ministry team was to develop counseling services for international students. I considered campus ministry as a possible career.

Increasingly, however, I focused on preparation for graduate work. I took a German-language course. While I never acquired competence to speak fluent German, I knew enough to be able to translate German material for my doctoral dissertation research. Years later, in 2014, I spent several weeks in Berlin doing research for a projected history of the International Fellowship of Reconciliation.

Among lasting influences of my seminary education were the friendships formed with Dr. Skoglund, Dr. Pemberton, and their partners. Dr. Skogland and his wife Daisy had a cottage near Rochester where they invited me to visit on several occasions. Eric Nelson recalled our relaxing there. The Skoglunds introduced us to the *Tarzan of the Jungle* novels. He also taught us to use an outrigger boat that John had imported from Thailand, plus a motor boat. Similarly, Pem and his wife Leota had a cottage accessed from Parry Sound, Ontario along the Georgian Bay of Lake Huron. Some years later, Nancy and I purchased a cottage on an island accessed from Pointe au Baril, a small town twenty-five miles to the north of Parry Sound.

Reflecting on my seminary education, I was prepared for ordination and ministry. I was well grounded for what proved to be forty years teaching in higher education, primarily in two seminaries. But easily the greatest contribution of my seminary years was having met my partner of nearly sixty years, Nancy Jean Rose, with whom I have truly shared life abundant.

21

Flower City Conspiracy

WHILE I WAS IN Rochester, a group known as the Flower City Conspiracy actively spoke out on the issues of racism, the war in Southeast Asia and the role of US government agencies whose offices the group disrupted before their arrest on September 6, 1970. Eight members of the Flower City Conspiracy were put on trial and faced possible sentences of up to thirty-eight years.[1]

Their trial took place in November in Federal Court. In solidarity, I joined a vigil in support of their defence. Despite compelling testimony of the Jesuit priest Daniel Berrigan and others, the defendants were convicted of hindering the Selective Service system, damaging FBI and Selective Service property, removing Selective Service and US Attorney files, breaking, and entering.

The trial of the Flower City Conspiracy defendants helped me clarify my opposition to the war. As a way to publicize their goals and to raise funds for their defence, a group of us did a reading of Daniel Berrigan's *The Trial of the Catonsville Nine*. The play detailed an action in May 1968 by Daniel Berrigan, his brother Philip and seven other Catholics at Catonsville, a Baltimore, Maryland suburb. The group burnt draft records. In several performances of

---

1. Barry Wingard, "The Trial of the Flower City Conspiracy," *Harvard Crimson* December 2, 1970 available at https://www.thecrimson.com/article/1970/12/2/the-trial-of-the-flower-city/.

the play, I read Thomas Melville's lines. As well, I wrote letters and met with my representatives in Congress to express my opposition to the war. I twice joined groups that traveled to Washington, D. C. for rallies against the war.

Recently, Ted Glick, one of the Flower City Conspiracy defendants, has published *Burglar for Peace* in which he describes the Rochester action. Reviewing the book in the *National Catholic Reporter*, Marie Dennis writes,

> So, I found *Burglar for Peace* to be both interesting and informative. But, from the perspective of my current work — with Pax Christi International's Catholic Nonviolence Initiative — I believe that the book's deepest value is in Glick's concluding look at the effectiveness of different nonviolent strategies in our current context, where imagining and "living our way into" a new, more just "normal" will require that we build organizations and communities that truly reflect the life-giving values we claim to believe.[2]

In 1967, I gave up the security of an educational deferment from the draft and applied to the Selective Service System to be classified as a conscientious objector. I met with my draft board in person. During the interview, I self-identified as a pacifist but acknowledged that some situations may require physical force to restrain evil. My draft board granted me c.o. status and accepted my service in Cameroon with the US Department of State as alternative service.

By supporting the Flower City Conspiracy, I believed that I was contributing to efforts to end the Vietnam war, to mobilize against other wars, and to generate communities of hope that reflect the life-affirming values that I believed to be foundational for the future of humanity. By resisting war preparation and a specific conflict, sometimes through civil disobedience, I had come to understand that we must wage peace in order that I and others might enjoy life abundant.

---

2. For a review, https://www.ncronline.org/news/book-reviews/book-chronicles-reckless-courage-catholic-resistance-vietnam-war.

22

Foreign Service Officer

APPLYING TO SERVE WITH the Department of State involved two parts. An exam tested a candidate's knowledge of US history and culture. An interview followed. The seasoned officers asked such questions as, "Who are your favorite American authors?" I replied, "Jack London and Eugene Burdick." "And poets?" "Emily Dickinson and Walt Whitman."

At the conclusion of the interview, I was told that I was an "interesting candidate" and that the Foreign Service was recruiting to its diplomatic corps individuals who could help realize some of the visionary elements of the administrations of Presidents Kennedy and Johnson. After a process that included police clearance and vetting of my future partner. I was invited to join the foreign service.

I spent June-December 1967 in orientation and French-language study. I lived in Arlington, Virginia, a short walk from the Department of State offices. The National Cemetery was also nearby. I often visited the John F. Kennedy Eternal Flame, the memorial at the gravesite of the assassinated US president.

While orienting with the US Department of State, new FSOs were urged to call on their Congressional representatives. I met Republican Senator George Murphy. I used the opportunity to support creation of a Redwood National Park. Senator Murphy thought the trees were useful primarily for fences and picnic tables. I was more appreciative of my brief visit with my House representative, Jerome Waldie, a Democrat who was an early critic of US involvement in the Vietnam War and an advocate for health care reform. Congressman Waldie followed up by writing my parents to congratulate them on my appointment.

After completing my French-language course, Nancy and I married and proceeded to Yaoundé, the French-speaking capital of Cameroon in West Africa. Working in the rarefied world of international diplomacy, I could walk to the embassy from a US government owned house where Nancy began our married life.

Yaoundé was a relatively small post. As a consular official, I issued passports for US citizens and visas for visitors to the US. I developed friendly relations with Cameroonians involved in government, academics, mining, and exports like cocoa, coffee, tea, and tropical fruits.

Perhaps my favorite role was to administer a self-help fund to promote the well-being of Cameroonians. I received and assessed proposals and approved grants. One permitted a village to create a co-operative to facilitate the export of crops. Another enabled villager to install a water-purification system and better latrines. When describing my work, I spoke of providing funds for a credit union in Kikakalaki and clean water in Guzang. I also undertook special assignments such as preparing for the visit of William Pierce Rogers, who served as Secretary of State during the Nixon administration.

After I completed my two-year assignment to Yaoundé, Nancy and I lived several months in Douala, the commercial capital of the country. I served as Consul. In this role, I had to clear through customs materials for the construction of a rail line extending from the north of the country to Douala. One of the purposes of Secretary Rogers' visit was to dedicate this major foreign assistance aided project.

Typically, there were glitches. During my intake interview, I had been asked if I would ever bribe anyone. Of course not, I replied. Yet, as Secretary Rogers' visit neared, equipment for the rail project was held-up at customs. To lubricate the process, I offered an official a red bottle of Johnny Walker Scotch. He replied, *Non, monsieur, noir, non rouge* (no, sir, black label, not red). I complied.

Another responsibility was servicing US interests in Fernando Po, which was still a Spanish colony. Having visited the island as a Crossroader in 1965, I returned to the territory in an official capacity. As in Cameroon, I approved applications that provided funds for life-enhancing projects promoting community health.

As our time in Cameroon neared completion, I pondered my future with the US Department of State. Two ambassadors, Robert Payton and Lewis Hoffacker, regarded my work highly. Each annual review was positive. I received two promotions and had every expectation of a successful career. I could imagine one day being named an ambassador or Assistant Secretary of State.

However, I was deeply troubled by US foreign policy, especially regarding priorities in terms of development assistance and the deepening US military engagement in South East Asia. I shared these concerns with Ambassadors Payton and Hoffacker, and with then Secretary of State Rogers during his visit to Cameroon.

I understood that, while there is a place in the diplomatic service to imagine foreign policy alternatives and to submit recommendations, nonetheless, I was obligated to represent decisions made at the highest level of government. Unable to support US policies towards Southeast Asia, I took a leave of absence, during which I completed the Master of Divinity degree at CRDS.

After graduation, I returned to Washington, D. C. and served briefly as assistant to Deputy Secretary of State, Alan Anderson Reich with the Bureau of Educational and Cultural Affairs. Learning of my likely assignment to Vienna, Austria in the area of disarmament and arms control, I faced a choice between two divergent roads as in Robert Frost's "The Road Not Taken."

After much reflection, I resigned, returned to school and ultimately undertook a teaching career. In December 1996, I returned to Cameroon for a month with MTS students in an immersion course. I visited the embassy and chatted with François, who had been my assistant and still worked there. I also met the US ambassador, Charles H. Twining, Jr ., who asked why I had resigned. I explained. Ambassador Twining responded that US policies would have been more fruitful had my vision prevailed.

My initial overseas experiences in Chad and Cameroon proved invaluable in my professional development, notably by instilling in me a sense of being part of a global community. Recognizing that my abundant life owed much from the legacy of European colonialism, I strove to find ways to promote a greater common good.

As well, my experience in West Africa introduced me to Muslims and adherents of traditional African religions. I established friendships, some of which I retained for decades. And I made a contribution to the lives of others, notably Chadian counterparts who worked with our Crossroads Africa team and Cameroonians who benefitted concretely from the foreign aid projects I administered. Such commitment to work for a better, more peaceful, and just world has remained a primary focus of abundance in my life.

23

Ministry and Ordination

SHORTLY AFTER ARRIVING IN Yaoundé, Cameroon in early 1968, Nancy and I attended an English-language service held in the chapel of a seminary training future Cameroonian ordinands. David Gelzer, a missionary with the Presbyterian Church (USA), or Geoffrey Wainwright, an English Methodist missionary, preached on alternating Sundays.

After Nancy and I had been in the country a few months, the Gelzer and Wainwright families departed on home leave. As I had had theological training, I was asked if I would step into the breach on an interim basis. I agreed and served the congregation on a limited basis for two years. I preached and led Sunday school but did not perform other duties (pastoral care, weddings, and funerals) that I felt inconsistent with my position with the US government.

The English-language service of the national radio station broadcast my sermons. When I returned to Cameroon in 1996 as part of a MTS immersion course, I visited the station and listened to a tape of one sermon.

During the 1970–1971 academic year, I completed a Master of Divinity degree at CRDS. For my field placement, I served as an assistant to Hays Rockwell, ecumenical chaplain at the University of Rochester. An Episcopal priest who went on to become ninth bishop of the Episcopal Diocese of Missouri, Hays provided spiritual direction as I wrestled with my future.

That Spring, I sought ordination through South Avenue Baptist Church, which organized a gathering of the Monroe Baptist Association of the American Baptist Churches. I have appended an excerpted text of the paper I prepared for the council that led to my ordination on May 5, 1971. Gordon Kurtz preached at the service. Gordon generally read a manuscript. On this occasion, speaking without notes, he drew from Acts 5:29. Peter said, "We must obey God rather than any human authority." Mitzi Collins, my colleague at the University of Rochester, led the music, which included singing "Simple Gifts," from the Shaker tradition, and a Beatles song.

Nancy and I were uncertain as to our future. Overseas ministry through the American Baptist denomination or teaching were possibilities. Further education was necessary. I applied to several doctoral programs and was accepted by three: Yale University, the Graduate Theological Union at Berkeley, and the University of Chicago. I visited each campus and talked with my prospective faculty advisors.

Still hesitant, I also consulted my Christian history professor Winthrop Hudson. As he . reflected on my decision, "Win" removed his glasses, paused—I was suspended in uncertainty—and then announced he would call Martin E. Marty at the University of Chicago to affirm my acceptance there.

At Chicago, I continued in ministry as youth director at an American Baptist congregation. After a year, I resigned because I realized I would not complete my doctoral program unless I was fully engaged to finish my doctorate within a reasonable time frame.

Committed to service abroad, Nancy and I considered an appointment to teach through American Baptist international ministries at a seminary in Zaire. Perhaps by serendipity, nationalist sentiment there precluded the possibility of our receiving visas. Subsequently, my formal ministry involved theological education, which enhanced my life abundant.

24

Graduate School

MY TIME AT THE University of Chicago enabled me to study with excellent scholars, some of whom became mentors and friends. Courses with each member of the church history faculty—Robert M. Grant, Bernard McGinn, Jerald C. Brauer, B. A. Gerrish, and Martin E. Marty—enabled me successfully to pass Masters and Doctoral exams and, perhaps more important—to cover the whole field of Christian history in case I ended up in a teaching career.

Martin Emil Marty (1928-2025), professor of Christian history, was my supervisor.[1] In addition to courses he taught, Dr. Marty influenced my writing. I remember submitting my thesis proposal to him for scrutiny. After reading the page, he swung around to his typewriter (yes, this was a pre-computer era) and succinctly summarized the manuscript in a paragraph.

Ralph A. Austen (1937-2024), an African history specialist whom Nancy and I had met while he did research in Cameroon,

---

1. Dr. Marty's work explored the intersections of faith, culture, and society. In my library, I have seminal books by him. Several continue to shape my academic interests including *Righteous Empire*, *Modern American Religion*, and *Fundamentalisms Observed*. As well, Dr. Marty was long-time editor of the journal *Christian Century*. Years later at a Thomas Merton-related gathering at which I co-presented a paper with Gary Purdy, former dean of engineering at McMaster, I introduced Gary to Dr. Marty who took a sheet from his pocket and showed Gary my name among over a hundred students he had mentored.

was a crucial member of my thesis committee.[2] Adviser and friend, Dr. Austin and I played tennis or sometimes lunched together. I also enjoyed the opportunity to study with members of the History of Religions stream: Mircea Eliade, Frank Reynolds, and Charles H. Long. I also had courses with renowned anthropologists, Victor Turner and Mary Douglas. In courses with David Tracy, I read *Pedagogy of the Oppressed* by the Brazilian educator Paulo Freire and *A Theology of Liberation* by the Peruvian Gustavo Gutiérrez. These thinkers introduced me to liberation theology, which has continued to shape my social activism.

In addition to Cameroon-related courses with Dr. Austen, I studied African history at Northwestern University. I worked with my church history mentors as their editorial assistant for the journal *Church History*. This experience fine tuned my writing. As well, I gained contacts with authors who submitted articles and reviews for possible publication.

Living in the Hyde Park neighborhood of Chicago, we had easy access to shops, notably, the Practical Tiger where we bought needed furniture that we still have. We traveled throughout the city to visit must-see tourist sites.

Chicago proved to be a kid-friendly for our son Nathaniel. We lived within easy walking or biking distance to a beach on Lake Michigan. On one occasion, I parked my bike with Nathaniel still in the child seat. He squirmed sufficiently to end up in a bush. We visited attractions such as the Children's Museum, Lincoln Park Zoo, the Shedd Aquarium, Adler Planetarium, and the Griffin Museum of Science and Industry. We watched a few baseball games at the White Sox stadium Comiskey Park or the Cubs' Wrigley Field. We ate out from time to time at Uno Pizzeria's deep-dish pizza, The Bergoff, a downtown German restaurant, or the Greek Isles. Nathaniel enjoyed throwing peanut shells onto the floor of a local pizzeria.

After I completed my Masters degree, I resided for a month at a Quaker study center, Pendel Hill in Wallingford, Pennsylvania from which I traveled to Presbyterian archives in Philadelphia for

---

2. https://news.uchicago.edu/story/ralph-austen-historian-africa-and-scholars-scholar-1937–2024 for an obituary.

dissertation research. My thesis project explored the impact of Presbyterian missionaries who worked among the Bulu of Cameroon. Over the next year, I wrote "Crossing Religious Frontiers. Christianity and the Transformation of Bulu (Cameroon) Society 1892–1925" and received my doctorate in early 1978.

When I returned to Chicago formally to receive my degree, I spoke with Brenda Gates, who had begun her studies at the same time I did. I expressed surprise that I had finished ahead of her. She observed that, alarmed by the length of time many students required to complete a Ph.D., I had seemed especially determined to finish the degree in four years and get on with life.

Through my time at the University of Chicago, I grew intellectually. Nancy, Nathaniel, and I enjoyed our time in the city. This period of growth enhanced my life abundant. When I applied for teaching positions, references from my committee members opened doors to a forty-year teaching career which has been very much a part of my life abundant.

25

Teaching and Sabbaticals

I BEGAN MY TEACHING career during the 1975–1976 academic year as an Instructor of Religion at Central Michigan University in Mt. Pleasant, Michigan. I joined an excellent faculty with Stan Walters, chair and a biblical scholar; Ken Folkert, a specialist in Asian religion; Mathias Zahniser, a specialist in Islamic studies; and Marybeth Rupert, a specialist in North American religious studies.

That year, in addition to teaching experience and developing good friendships, Nancy, Nathaniel, and I worshipped with a small Quaker community. We enjoyed weekend trips, especially opportunities to camp along the shores of Lake Michigan.

During the Summer of 1976, a CMU colleague provided me an office where I would not be bothered. This enabled me to complete revisions of my doctoral thesis. Although CMU offered me a tenure-track position, I had a similar offer at McMaster University.

Wrestling with yet another vocational decision, I again found Nancy especially helpful in making the decision to accept the McMaster position. One consideration for this choice was the opportunity to teach both university, and seminary courses. Another factor was the chance to move to Canada. Over the years, Nancy and I had visited Bayfield, Ontario, where the Kurtz family had a Summer cottage. We were impressed by Canada's commitment to provide all residents comprehensive medical care and other social services. Finally, there were wider issues. Officially, Canada had not sent troops to support US intervention in Vietnam and was prepared to abolish the death penalty. Such concerns contributed to our decision to move to Canada.

As Labour Day and the start of the academic year approached, Nancy, Nathaniel, and I had not yet received visas to enter Canada. I visited the Canadian consulate in Detroit to ascertain why we had not yet received our visas and learned we had not yet received security clearance. I supposed this may have arisen from my having participated in nonviolent civil disobedience actions in Berkeley and Rochester.

I called Ivan Morgan, then principal of McMaster Divinity College, who in turn contacted Fraser Fell, then chair of the Board of Governors of McMaster University who helped clear the way for us to enter Canada. During our early years in Canada, many regarded me as one of the Vietnam war resisters who entered Canada to avoid being drafted. Expressing respect for such conscientious objection, I stressed that my family and I came to Canada through the usual immigration process.

I taught at McMaster for nearly twenty years with a dual appointment as Professor of Church History at McMaster Divinity College and Professor of Theology in McMaster University. In the mid-1980s, I became the first Centenary Professor of World Christianity in the Divinity College. A campaign on the occasion of McMaster's hundredth anniversary funded this new position.

Early in my teaching career, I developed several foci that reflected my view that education should be practical and engage students in the wider world. One component development of courses with an immersion experience in various cultural contexts. I chose communities where students were able to live in the community and get to know residents. At McMaster, I organized four such courses. One involved Native Canadians. Another focused on New Canadians. Two other immersion courses involved a month each in India (1987) and Bolivia (1993). These were part of celebrations of the centenary of Canadian Baptist witness in the respective countries.

Another concentration was peace studies. In the early 1980s, I joined scholars from throughout McMaster University in efforts to establish a Centre for Peace Studies. Its creation was inspired partly by the work of the Peace Research Institute, co-founded in Dundas by Alan and Hannah Newcombe. With support from Alvin A. Lee, President and Vice-Chancellor of McMaster from 1980 to 1990, we formed an ad-hoc Committee for Canada-Latin American Friendship. Our first initiative was a visit to campus of Adolpho Perez Esquivel, the 1980 Nobel Peace Prize laureate.

I recognized my need to develop knowledge about peace studies in an area of conflict. To this end, and, in addition, to deepen my knowledge of my family roots, I chose Israel as a setting for my first sabbatical. Our family lived at Tantur, an ecumenical center on the Jerusalem-Bethlehem road. My primary research concerned the Israel-Palestine conflict. I interviewed widely and took courses in the English-language program of Hebrew University.

Upon return, I co-taught an introductory course in the field of peace studies with Graeme MacQueen, a colleague in the Department of Religious Studies, and Joanna Santa Barbara, a child psychiatrist and member of McMaster's medical faculty. I also taught a course on Issues in War and Peace, offered jointly by the Religious Studies Department and McMaster Divinity College.[1]

Over the next few years, our ad hoc committee developed other peace studies courses taught in several McMaster University departments. These courses drew, and continue to attract large enrollments.[2] We also undertook public education initiatives, including the Bertrand Russell Peace Lectures, the Mahatma Gandhi Lectures on Nonviolence, and conferences on areas such as peace

---

1. Gordon L. Heath succeeded me as Professor of Christian History and Centenary Professor of World Christianity in the Divinity College. On occasion, he has invited me to lecture in one of his classes. He autographed my copy of an anthology he edited, *Canadian Churches and the First World War*, "To Paul, May God bless your continued efforts for peace. Your friend, Gord Heath."

2. Speier, ed., *Canadian Peace and World Order Studies. A Curriculum Guide*, 145–48 and 528–32 for the syllabi of "Introduction to the Study of Peace" and "Issues in War and Peace."

advocacy and social justice. In 1989, the University Senate approved creation of the Centre for Peace Studies (now called Global Peace and Social Justice) and a Combined Honours Bachelor of Arts program with a Minor in Peace Studies.

During the 1991–1992 academic year, I served as Director of the program. In this capacity, I helped write a grant application for which the Centre and McMaster's medical faculty received a grant for nearly two and a half million dollars from the Canadian Government.

These funds were awarded in the context of Canada's ratification in 1991 of the United Nations Convention on the Rights of the Child. The Peace through Health grant enabled us to establish a multidisciplinary program on civilian and child health and to fund projects in Sri Lanka, El Salvador, the Palestinian Occupied Territories, and former Yugoslavia. As our three-year government grant came to an end, the projects developed their own funding. At least one, in Sri Lanka, continues through a peace garden.

In recognition of my contribution to "universal peace, justice, and world citizenship" the Hamilton Mundialization Committee presented me in 1994, a World Citizenship Award. I display a plaque from this accolade in my office.

During this same period, I was involved in raising funding for a new position at the seminary and was inaugurated as professor of world Christianity in the late 1980s. Along with Al Roxburgh as Director, we launched a Centre for Mission and Evangelism and found a great deal of support for the initiative both from faculty colleagues and in the wider Baptist denomination. Twenty years later, I occasionally worship, preach, or lead workshops in Baptist congregations, during which participants recall seminars or sermons that I offered through the Centre for Mission and Evangelism.

During my latter years at McMaster Divinity College, I was deeply troubled by what I understood as a resumption of the modernist/fundamentalist spat of the early twentieth century. In the 1980s, the board McMaster Divinity College and its host denomination reflected a more conservative trend of among Baptists.

Reflective of this shift, a noted conservative, Clark Pinnock, was appointed to the chair of theology, and John Irwin, a publisher and well-known evangelical, became board chair.

In 1987, I was especially alarmed by the appointment of William Brackney as successor to Mel Hillmer as MDC principal. I was not surprised that, during Dr. Brackney's tenure, several faculty members moved to other institutions. Al Roxburgh accepted a pastoral call in Vancouver. Ray Hobbs, a biblical scholar, went to a Baptist seminary in the Czech Republic. Several faculty members retired or were forced to resign. I accepted a position at Memphis Theological Seminary.

In a study of Canadian evangelicalism in the 1990s, Queen's University historian George Rawlyk cited an article in *Christian Week* entitled "The Unlikely Transformation of McMaster Divinity College." The original article stated, "something incongruous and largely unexpected" was happening at the school. MDC, long berated in conservative circles as a bastion of modernism, is now earning a reputation as an increasingly evangelical school."[3]

Looking back at the changes that were impacting McMaster Divinity College in the late 1980s, and early 1990s I came to see this as a case study in an anthropology course I took at the University of Chicago. We read Mary Douglas, *Purity and Danger,* in which she explored how ideas about separating, purifying, demarking, and punishing transgressions have as their main function imposing order on an inherently untidy experience.[4]

Extrapolating from this analysis, I came to understand that some members of the board of the Divinity College, believing the seminary had abandoned its more evangelical, or conservative roots, were committed to reversing the so-called liberal direction of many faculty members. As some members of the board and wider denomination determined that it was imperative to return the seminary to its place as a major evangelical institution, they resolved to purify the school, along with the wider denomination and thus avoid what they considered "a deadly virus—the

---

3. Rawlyk, *In Search of Canadian Evangelicalism,* 46.
4. Douglas, *Purity and Danger,* 15

powerful tendency to adjust the sacred to meet the demands of worldly success."[5]

As working conditions at the seminary became more and more uncomfortable, Nancy and I weighed various options. Initially, I considered applying for positions elsewhere, but timing was awkward. In 1991–1992, I was administrating the Peace through Health grant for which I had significant responsibility.

As well, I served on two Canadian Council of Churches (CCC) commissions—the Peace and Justice Commission and Middle East Working Group—two Baptist World Alliance committees, and the boards of several organizations, including an Amnesty International group that I chaired at McMaster University. My teaching, research, wider activity, and family life were deeply satisfying. This made it difficult to consider moving at the time.

In the Fall of 1994, my congregation MacNeill Baptist Church hosted a meeting of the BPFNA board, on which I represented Canadian Baptists. Paula Womack, a staff member and MTS student, urged me to apply for an open position at MTS with a focus on the legacy of the Reverend Dr. Martin Luther King, Jr.

I sought the advice of several friends, notably John and Joan Robertson. Joan was born and raised in Memphis. John had taught in the Deep South. Both were aware of my dis-ease with developments at McMaster Divinity College. Both were enormously affirming of the possibility of a new start in Memphis. Some years later, John taught as an adjunct for MTS during which time Joan audited my Thomas Merton course, which included a week's retreat at the Abbey of Gethsemani.

After a process of discernment, I recognized I could no longer support the direction the seminary was taking. I applied for the MTS position. During my interview, then President J. David Hester, asked why I would leave a tenured position in which I had clearly thrived. I replied, "I just turned fifty." He responded, "I understand." Later, I learned that at age fifty, he had left a pastorate to accept the MTS presidency, in which position he served from 1984–1997.

---

5. Rawlyk, *In Search of Canadian Evangelicalism*, 47.

Teaching and Sabbaticals

I taught full time in Memphis from January 1995 until 2008 in the academic area of evangelism and mission, a new academic discipline for me. At the time of my appointment, in addition to President David Hester, Don McKim served as academic dean. Steve Parish and Mitzi Minor taught biblical studies. W. E. "Knick" Knickerbocker taught Christian history. Paul Blankenship taught Methodist studies. Mary Lin Hudson taught homiletics and liturgics. Jay Earheart-Brown was appointed in the area of theology and soon became president. Subsequently, Lee Ramsey taught pastoral theology and preaching. Robert Stanley Wood taught African-American studies and later became dean.

In addition to an excellent faculty, our student body was larger and more diverse than that at McMaster Divinity College. As well, in addition to teaching a course on Dr. King for MTS students, I was asked to offer courses for the Communications Department of the University of Memphis on the Rhetoric of Martin Luther King, Jr. and the Rhetoric of Women in the Civil Rights Movement. As an adjunct at the University of Memphis, I supervised doctoral projects of two Cameroonians in the area of African history. In 2008, when I retired from full-time teaching, MTS named me Professor Emeritus in which role I continued to teach as an adjunct for several years thanks in part to a donation to the seminary by my sister.

Moving to Memphis, Tennessee had enormous implications for our family. During my first term, January-May 1995, Nancy remained in Hamilton. She joined me in the Fall of 1995 and was able to transfer her nursing credentials and find employment. During the 1995–1996 academic year, our sons Nathaniel and Matthew cared for our Hamilton home while they completed their school years. Nathaniel ultimately remained in Hamilton, while Matthew enrolled at Rhodes College in Memphis from which he graduated in 2000.

Among many highlights of our Memphis years was the development of enduring friendships with two MTS colleagues, Mary Lin Hudson and Mitzi Minor, and several community members, Annie Beckham, Faith Barcroft, Eyleen Farmer, and Tom Momberg.

On several occasions, we have travelled to vacation places of great beauty including the Grand Canyon, Arizona; Bryce and Zion National Parks and Escalante National Monument in Utah; the Cape Breton Trail in Nova Scotia; the Canadian Rockies; coastal Maine; Ashville, North Carolina at the start of the Appalachian Trail; in 2023, Livingston, Montana along the Yellowstone River, famed site for the 1992 film *A River Runs Through It*. Fly-fishing enthusiasts, Mary Lin Hudson and I tried our luck several times through the week. We failed to catch a single fish.

Just in advance of sending this manuscript to the publisher, our group undertook yet another adventure. We explored the southern half of Vancouver Island in British Columbia, where we enjoyed Butchart Gardens, ocean highways, museums, provincial parks and, most significantly, time together.

My teaching career had the benefit offered by few professions, namely sabbaticals every seventh year. I have already mentioned our first sabbatical year in Israel (1982–1983). We lived at an Ecumenical Institute known as Tantur, on the road from Jerusalem to Bethlehem. Associated with Notre Dame University, the institution continues to offer continuing education and sabbatical programs for Christians seeking to deepen their faith in the Holy Land.

Through an interweaving of lectures and excursions, generally organized by an American Baptist missioner, Wesley Brown, we encountered the sacredness of the region's geography, history and complex religious traditions. In addition to lectures, Dr. Geries Sa'ed Khoury, a Tantur scholar and team-member in the Christianity in the Holy Land Program, offered an introduction to Arabic. During our second term, Tantur hosted a sabbatical opportunity for several Maryknoll missionaries whose sojourn enriched our experience.

For the academic year, Nathaniel enrolled in an Anglican school that enabled him to further his French-language study. Matthew attended pre-kindergarten in a school run by Finnish missionaries. I took advantage of the English language program at Hebrew University by auditing a course on rabbinic teaching and

Teaching and Sabbaticals

another on the Palestine-Israel conflict. Nancy walked or took a bus weekly to Bethlehem where she volunteered at an orphanage run by nuns.

Tantur's director, Donald Nicholl drew on his service in Burma during World War II. He had a profound understanding of conflict and, among initiatives, created a series of lectures on the possession and use of nuclear weapons in the light of Torah, Gospel, and Sharia.

Donald profoundly influenced Nancy's and my understanding of peace, justice and reconciliation. In addition to *The Beatitude of Truth. Reflections of a Lifetime* and other books, he wrote a regular column for *The Tablet*, an English religious periodical. In one article, "Saints for Peace," he urged the need to acknowledge that every faith is judged in the light of the highest teachings and exemplars, "peace saints" awakened to live with compassion and peacemaking. As peace saints, Donald and his wife Dorothy strove to bind the broken human family together.[6]

For my second sabbatical (1991–1992), I affiliated with a Baptist-related Regent's Park College located at the heart of Oxford, England. Researching Baptist history, I wrote *For the Healing of the Nations: Baptist Peacemakers* for which my thesis supervisor, Martin E. Marty, contributed a Forward. My onetime pastor and friend, Nancy Hastings Sehested, wrote a preface.

In January 1995, when I began teaching at Memphis Theological Seminary, I was nearing time for another sabbatical and had already agreed to an exchange with a member of the faculty of Whitley College of Melbourne University in Australia. MTS granted my request for an early sabbatical during the Spring 1998 term. This third sabbatical proved to be the first of eight opportunities to teach at Whitley. On one of these visits to Australia, a Whitley colleague and biblical scholar Keith Dyer taught a term at MTS.

I spent a fourth sabbatical at two locations. During the Fall 2001 term, I resided at a Church of the Brethren institution, Elizabethtown College in Lancaster County, Pennsylvania in order to

---

6. Nicholl, "Saints for Peace," *Tablet*, January 4, 1992, 8–9; https://tantur.org/ for information about the institute.

learn about one of the three historic peace churches that, along with Quakers and Mennonites, contributed significantly to the Fellowship of Reconciliation about which I was writing.

Elizabethtown was close to the Three Mile Island accident site where in 1979 a nuclear reactor released radioactive gases and radioactive iodine into the environment. Donald B. Kraybill, who provided a Foreword for *Creating the Beloved Community*, written that term, and other Elizabethtown residents recalled having been warned to pull down shades over windows, which could not have protected residents from adverse health effects resulting from the accident.

During the Spring 2002 term, Nancy and I resided at St. Johns Abbey in Collegeville, Minnesota. The abbey came to our attention through reading *The Cloister Walk* by Kathleen Norris. My sabbatical project concerned the Cistercian monk Thomas Merton, who recalled his visit to St. Johns in one of his journals.[7] Monks passed on oral legend that Merton almost drowned in Stump Lake, a story that he did not record in his journal. This seemed similar to tales shared by Gethsemani monks who described Merton as the "absent-minded professor" who crashed the monastery jeep and nearly killed himself while felling trees with novices.[8] This research contributed to courses, talks, papers, and two books about Merton.

Throughout my experience as a teacher of Christian pastors and religious educators, I have stressed the importance of continuing education. Throughout my teaching career, such sabbatical research and writing have nurtured me. Continuing education thus contributed enormously to my life abundant.

---

7. Merton journaled about his time at St. John's Abbey in *A Search for Solitude*, 54–62.

8. Emails, Paul M. Pearson, Director of the Thomas Merton Center at Bellarmine University in Louisville, Kentucky and Chief of Research for the Merton Legacy Trust, and his associate, Mark Meade, January 23, 2025.

26

Religious Communities

I HAD MAINTAINED MEMBERSHIP in Baptist congregations since my teen years. In September 1971, when Nancy and I moved to Chicago, we initially worshipped at a Baptist congregation. I volunteered as mentor for a youth group. On one occasion, we had an evening program. Because lights were on, a police officer stopped by and confirmed that everything was ok. It was!

A member of the congregation learned that a policeman had stopped at the church and concluded we had caused trouble of some sort. Ridiculous. The officer had noticed that there were lights left on in the building and simply checked if there was any difficulty. Nonetheless, alarmed by the lack of support by some congregants, I resigned. For the duration of our Chicago years, Nancy and I worshipped at the 57th Street Meeting of the Religious Society of Friends.

Initially during our Hamilton years, Nancy and I joined MacNeill Baptist Church. We appreciated the preaching and pastoral care of its pastor Bob Yanke and the Christian education program shared with a neighboring congregation, Westdale United Church. Successor pastors have continued to offer fine leadership. In addition to a strong music program, the congregation has long been a welcoming and affirming community with no barriers to participation across the spectrums of human identity or sexual orientation.

In the 1980s, a Canadian Baptist peace group began to meet. We put forward resolutions before the Baptist Convention of Ontario and Quebec. We held an annual retreat at Ganaraska Woods, a facility of Calvary Baptist Church in Toronto. One of our members, John Sabean, edited a newsletter, the *Baptist Peace Link*. John was a trained historian, co-founder of our group, and a tireless advocate for heritage preservation. The newsletter provided an outlet for our vision.

In the early 1990s, I helped initiate a parallel group, the Gathering of Baptists, which mobilized against the direction McMaster Divinity College and the wider denomination had taken. Now affiliated with the wider BPFNA, the Gathering has provided me an opportunity to connect with former students and new friends twice a year. As well, it has provided a recognized body through which I retain ordination credentials.

In the 1980s and early 1990s, I was part of a group that met weekly for prayer at Welcome Inn, a community center in a poor neighborhood of Hamilton. Having experienced meditative prayer in other contexts, I appreciated our hour of silent worship. This led me to suggest that MacNeill offer such an opportunity. In response, our pastor Bob Yanke introduced a brief period of silence in the regular Sunday morning worship. This proved something of an awakening for me, as some congregants did not appreciate this innovation and ultimately left.

Having been introduced to Quaker worship some years earlier, I sought a community more open to spirituality rooted in silence, stillness, and solitude. From time to time, I attended Sunday morning worship at the Hamilton Meeting of the Religious Society of Friends (Quakers) and ultimately became a member of the community.

In 1995, when Nancy and I moved to Memphis, Tennessee, we initially attended Prescott Memorial Baptist Church. Its pastor, Nancy Hastings Sehested and her husband, Ken—at the time, BPFNA executive director—were friends. Nancy had been the first woman called to a Southern Baptist affiliated congregation, an action that led the Shelby County Baptist Association to remove Prescott from membership.

When we considered membership at Prescott, the Sehesteds alerted us that we should not make a decision based on their leadership. They soon moved to North Carolina. Nancy had a vital ministry as a prison chaplain. Ken provided myriad resources invaluable for the wider peace movement. And together they co-pastored Circle of Mercy, a congregation related to the Alliance of Baptists.[1]

Among Nancy Sehested's successors at Prescott, Martha Brahm served several years. Nancy and I supported her ministry and volunteered with social outreach of the congregation. After Martha moved to Hawaii, Prescott merged with a Presbyterian congregation.

During our Memphis years, Nancy and I participated in servant leadership formation modeled on the Church of the Saviour in Washington D. C. On Saturdays, we could worship with members of the Servant Leadership school, and continue, on Sundays, to attend Prescott's worship.

As well, in Memphis, I began to attend the Memphis Meeting of the Religious Society of Friends. It had relocated two blocks from our home. Returning to Hamilton in 2008, Nancy and I continued worshipping with Quakers. I formally joined the Hamilton congregation for which I have served in many capacities including Recording Clerk (or secretary), clerk (or chair) of our Peace and Social Action Committee, liaison with the Canadian Friends Service Committee and as a member of CFSC's Israel-Palestine Working Group.

Among distinctives of my professional career has been a commitment to building ecumenical relationships. At McMaster Divinity College, I urged transition of the seminary from being almost exclusively Baptist to a more diverse faculty and student body. We hired non-Baptist faculty and recruited students more widely.

---

1. Nancy Sehested's *Marked for Life: A Prison Chaplain's Story* and Ken Sehested's publications such as *Dreaming God's Dream* attest to their prophetic leadership in church and society.

During the 1980s, I represented the Baptist Convention of Ontario and Quebec on the Peace and Justice Commission and Middle East Working Group of the Canadian Council of Churches (CCC). Through these bodies, I contributed to wider ecumenical ministry, for example, by contributing to several documents, including *Position Paper on the Middle East: A Study Guide* (1990). The text, approved by the wider CCC board, called for a comprehensive settlement of the Israeli-Palestinian conflict, including self-determination leading possibly to establishing a sovereign Palestinian state, a prophetic stance that proved controversial, has yet to be realized, and remains essential to transform a conflict that has persisted since 1948 when Israel became an independent nation to a just and lasting peace for both Israelis and Palestinians.

In 1993, Stuart Brown completed his service as General Secretary of the Canadian Council of Churches. Several colleagues urged that I apply to succeed him. In my process of discernment, I learned the position involved a great deal of travel, a role that I felt was not suitable at a time that I was co-parenting a young family. Nor did I feel skilled in fund-raising. With the help of a student, I did a self-study of personal gifts. Fund-raising was not one! I did not apply.

Later, I served six years with the Christian Interfaith Reference Group (CIRG), a working group of CCC. During the 2018–2021 triennium, our priority was to nurture Christian-Muslim and Christian-Jewish relations. Continuing these engagements during 2021–2024 triennium, we added an additional focus on "Indigenous Spiritualities in Canada: A Contribution to Reconciliation." As a significant part of our work, we met with a number of Christian indigenous spiritual leaders, generally by Zoom due to the Covid-19 pandemic.

On September 18–20, 2023, the CIRG had its first in-person meeting since the 2020–2021 epidemic made such gatherings impossible. We gathered at Friends' House in Toronto and appreciated the formal and informal connections and conversations at this gathering, especially since many of our newer members had not met one another in person before this meeting. Given our commitment to supporting indigenous communities, we also visited the Native Canadian Centre of Toronto.

As I came to an end of my second three-year term on CIRG, I felt that work remains to be done not only with this focus, but also with a second focus, the sin of racism. During the 2024–2027 triennium, CIRG is building on our work with particular consideration of how the sin of racism impacts relationships of all non-indigenous Canadians with First Nations, Metis and Inuit peoples. As CIRG members continue to wrestle with these issues, we have envisioned offering a resource of the same quality of prior CIRG documents to which I contributed including *Holy Day Greetings to Our Jewish Neighbours* (2021) and *Guide for Participation in Public Events Involving More than One Religious or Spiritual Tradition* (2021).

Challenged by this robust and important work, I have looked at my positive experience and experienced discouragement because Christian-Jewish and Israeli-Palestinian reconciliation remain so elusive. As I concluded my second three-year term representing Canadian Quakers on CIRG, I was pleased that CIRG members adopted as a priority during the 2024–2027 triennium, the sin of racism, with particular consideration of how the sin of racism impacts our relationships with First Nations, Inuit, and Metis people.

In its final report, the Truth and Reconciliation Commission of Canada called on church leaders and adherents to develop ongoing education strategies and projects to promote healing and partnership, a process that remains a priority agenda for me personally, for Hamilton Quakers, and for Canadians as a whole.

As I conclude this section, I express my gratitude to Canadian Quakers for naming me to serve on CIRG and to CCC staff member Maria Simakova, CCC General Secretary Peter Noteboom and colleagues representing other CCC churches for their commitment to ecumenical and interfaith work. In particular, I highlight my deep appreciation for having had the privilege to serve three years as co-chair with Roshni Jayawardena, an Anglican priest. Such work has contributed significantly to abundance in my life, and impacted countless others.

27

Servant Leadership

IN THE LATE 1940S, a Baptist pastor Gordon Cosby and a few others established the Church of the Saviour in Washington, D. C. The congregation described itself as follows,

> The revolutionary congregation is absolutely necessary to a revolutionary church in a revolutionary world. The congregation orients itself upon the world and upon the tasks which appear in the midst of the world. Its life is characterized by discipline and ecumenicity. The revolutionary church offers itself, its death, and life for the sake of the world in order to bring a future in which the possibilities for the fullness of human life are opened to all. To achieve this goal, the congregation must take a shape appropriate to the world's need, a shape of radical obedience to Christ. The shape of obedience is that of a task force, a revolutionary congregation gathered together for worship, study, and direct action in the world for the full realization of twentieth-century humanness.[1]

In 1967, living in Washington, D. C., I attended Sunday worship under Cosby's leadership. Mid-week, I participated in a servant leadership class. As a ministry opportunity, I served coffee or

---

1. For Cosby and O'Connor and the ministry, https://8th-day.org/core-documents/history-church-saviour.

Servant Leadership

tea at the Potter's House. I welcomed guests, received their order, and sat with them when invited to do so. Ever since, cappuccino has been my preferred specialty coffee.

During Memphis years, 1995–2008, Nancy and I participated in a Servant Leadership program. We developed the following mission statement:

> Being transformed toward the image of Christ through spiritual discipline and well-versed in the art of loving, well-grounded in committed community, committed to building relationships with persons who are poor, outcast and lost, committed to the transformation of the world through courageous and sacrificial living, our vision is to sponsor servant leaders who renew the church as servant in the world and, in so doing, recall us to our vocation as "the repairers of the breach and restorers of the streets to live in."[2]

In 2006, Ohne Johns, a member of our Servant Leadership group, took the lead in establishing Caritas Village. For her housing and a coffee-house ministry, she chose the name Caritas, Latin for "love for all people."

Caritas Village lives up to that love. It provides a place where friends break bread together and share conversation to nourish the body and soul. It is a cultural center and restaurant offering affordable, high-quality meals. When we have returned to Memphis, Nancy and I have observed how people from different backgrounds come together there to dine, share fun and create community.

Some people are troubled by the servant image. I too am leery of people who want to serve others. They are often motivated for the wrong reason. Some think that they are earning merit. Some respond to an inner voice of parents, "you have to do good." Some deprive grassroots organizations of the capacity to solve problems. Some violate a rule of empowerment, that one should never do for others what they can do for themselves. None of this has been my experience in either Washington, or Memphis servant leadership groups.

---

2. *Newsletter* (Winter 2001), cited in my *Holy Boldness*, 154. The text cited is Isaiah 58:12.

Life Abundant

In Memphis, I also volunteered with an ecumenical ministry, the Metropolitan Inter-Faith Association. I delivered meals-on-wheels. Similarly, returning to Canada, I have volunteered with Dundas Community Services through a "friendly calling" program.

This work involves telephoning senior clients on a pre-determined schedule, keeping records of calls, and reporting to the program coordinator concerns or changes in the status or health of clients. Since undertaking this work, I have telephoned a dozen seniors. I supported one callee by officiating a "celebration of life" for his deceased mother and brother. In another case, I attended a celebration of her life. Apart from her son and the minister who officiated, I was the only male in the room. After the service, her son asked who I was. I explained. He replied, "ah so you are Pavel (my name in Russian). Mother called me every week after your chats. I know your father was born in Chita, Siberia where, during the same period, my mother's father also worked." Yet another callee, a blues artist, has deepened into close friendship that nurtures my life abundant.

28

Monastic Journey

IN MY CHAPTER ON seminary education, I wrote briefly of a course on modern Catholicism with Dr. Winthrop Hudson, who encouraged me to visit a monastery. In response, I spent a few days at Mount Savior Monastery near Elmyra, New York.

After I accepted a teaching position at Memphis Theological Seminary I did a similar retreat at Gethsemani Abbey near Louisville, Kentucky, where the monk and writer Thomas Merton lived from 1941–1968. I learned that E. Glenn Hinson, Professor of Church History at Southern Baptist Theological Seminary occasionally brought a group of students to the monastery. With support of my MTS colleagues, I organized a similar course, a core component of which was a five-day retreat at the Abbey of Gethsemani. Before I retired from full-time teaching, I offered the course eight times The following is a brief account of the first retreat.

Early—5 a.m. early!—on Monday June 9, 1997, I gathered with a group of students in the seminary parking lot. Six hours later, we arrived for a five-day retreat at the Abbey of Gethsemani where I ceased to be course facilitator. I was a retreatant. For a few days, we observed the daily rhythm of work and prayer as outlined in the *Rule of St. Benedict*.

After morning prayers or in the afternoon, some of us on a voluntary basis joined the monks at work. I especially enjoyed evening prayers, or compline, a prayer for the loving protection of God through the night and at the unknown time of one's death. Usually chanted just before retiring, compline always included reading of Psalms 4, 91, and 134 and concluded with a blessing with holy water sprinkled on attendees by the abbot or abbess, prior or prioress.

As the daily schedule of the monks permitted, I walked along a path that meanders through the woods. I looked, listened, prayed, journaled, and photographed places associated with Merton, including a plot that preserves the outlines of his Zen garden and nearby shack, known as Saint Anne's. It served as Merton's first hermitage. There I could read notes left by other retreatants. They addressed such life situations as illness, decisions about vocation or life choices facing loved ones. In my own contribution to the notebook, I wrote, "the peace of Christ envelops me. The silence is wonderful. *Deo gratias!*"

On one occasion, after breakfast, one of the monks escorted me and a few other retreatants to the hermitage where Merton spent his last years. Over its door was the word, "Shalom," Hebrew for peace. A small sign adorned an empty chair on the porch with the words, "Bench of Dreams." Nearby were the wheel and cross often associated with the hermitage thanks to an iconic photograph taken by Merton.

On this and subsequent retreats at Gethsemani, I lingered for meditation at a garden with two large statues created by Walter Hancock in memory of Jonathan M. Daniels. An Episcopal seminarian and civil rights worker, Daniels was martyred in Alabama, August 20, 1965, when he stepped into a bullet intended for an African-American, Ruby Sales. A memorial plaque called on viewers always to remember that the church exists to lead people to Christ in many ways.[1]

---

1. A PBS presentation entitled "Here Am I, Send Me" explores Daniel's life and can be viewed on line. See www.bing.com/videos/riverview/relatedvideo?q=Here+Am+Ipercent2c+Send+Mepercent3a+The+Journey+of+Jonathan+Daniels&mid=AC0A34E99A0B59F52F80AC0A34E99A0B59F52F80&FORM=VIRE. Several Merton biographies are illustrated, including those by Michael Mott and Jim Forest.

Monastic Journey

During my Gethsemani retreats I had little direct contact with the MTS students. Through the week, we maintained silence on the monastery grounds, including the dining area and the oratory, the place of common prayer. On our journey home, students related their experience. Sharing fresh insights about monasticism and new understandings about their lives, students bubbled over with excitement.

Mid-way on our journey home, a storm with large hailstones pounded the van. So intense was the storm, we could not continue. The van stopped under an overpass. We climbed out of the crowded van for a stretch. Conversation continued as students shared their experience of an overflow of God's all-powerful presence.

Having moved only recently to Memphis, I was still struggling to accept my new situation. I asked, "Has God called me to Memphis to be a catalyst for this process?" I recognized that God had purpose for me in my new teaching milieu. Through this course, I had provided a small group, as well as myself an opportunity to be quiet, to rest, and to grow.

For me this was a simple lesson about living in the moment. I experienced enormous gratitude and freedom. I was at peace. With the monks and ten students as companions, I had found a way of living more deeply and humanely. In our world at a time of unprecedented challenges engendered by climate change, global migration, social injustice, and war, I came to believe that monasteries provide not only community members, but also devout laypeople hope, healing, and spiritual resources for everyday living.

In the 1930s, German theologian Dietrich Bonhoeffer anticipated the restoration of the church after the coming world war through a new kind of monasticism, a way of life of uncompromising adherence to the Sermon on the Mount in imitation of Christ. Since then, the renewal of Christian monasticism has become a great spiritual movement. Imbued with a love for God and neighbor, and with a healthy self-love, people are going to monasteries to deepen their relationship with God, to pray, and to find peace. While monastic vocations have declined in North America, many Christians are exploring alternative monastic

Life Abundant

lifestyles. As an outgrowth of our connection with a new monastic community in Australia, Nancy and I have endeavored to devote a period each morning for meditation. We sometimes follow a book of prayers and readings. On other occasions, we have read through the Psalms in various translations. Often, we light a candle and simply sit in quiet.[2]

Strengthened by praying, reading the *Bible*, practicing other spiritual disciplines, and monastic spirituality, I have also found an important teacher for me to be the Buddhist monk Thich Nhat Hahn who stresses the importance of practicing meditation, of seeking to acquire the capacity to look, to see and to understand. He writes, "Peace work means, first of all, being peace. Meditation is meditation for all of us. We rely on each other. Our children are relying on us in order for them to have a future."[3]

In September 2002, I served with a committee that invited Nhat Hanh to Memphis as part of a wider effort to protest the buildup of a US war in Iraq. I wrote an account of the visit of Nhat Hanh and other members of his community, published as "The Power of Silence," *Fellowship* 69 (January/February 2003) 15–16. One concrete outcome of PeaceWalk was creation of a hundred-and twenty-acre residential center to practice mindfulness. Nhat Hahn returned for the opening of Magnolia Grove Village near Batesville, Mississippi.[4] Ever since, it has served as a place of peace. After Nhat Hahn died, I wrote a tribute, published in *Fellowship* 83 (Spring 2020)12–14. As well as our daily devotion, Nancy and I have gone on many retreats. We have found meditation to be a crucial practice in our shared lives and in nurturing gratitude for lives of abundance.

---

2. One of the books Nancy and I have read is Judith Sutera's *Work of God. Benedictine Prayer*.

3. Hanh, *Being Peace*, 80.

4. https://magnoliagrovemonastery.org/plan-a-visit/.

29

Two Lakes

GROWING UP, I LOVED family vacations at Lake Tahoe on the California-Nevada border. Along with Lake Huron, where Nancy and I have our Summer cottage on an island in the Georgian Bay, these two bodies of water have provided the setting for some of my happiest memories and enhanced my life abundant.

At Tahoe, I enjoyed our drives around the lake's shoreline, Emerald Bay and national forest land surrounding the area that is laced with roads that offering stunning photography stops and opportunities to shop, dine, swim, or fish. As well, I enjoyed camping and hiking in the area.

As one example, during the Summer of 1964, I hiked south of Lake Tahoe along the John Muir Trail that runs along the High Sierras to Yosemite National Park with three of my closest friends, the late Don Jensen, Eric Nelson, and Alan Smith. We did about fifty miles (eighty kilometers) and carried incredible loads on our backs. According to a menu preserved in my copy of *Starr's Guide to the High Sierra Region of the John Muir Trail*, we ate well. Freshly-caught trout often complemented tuna casseroles, chipped beef sandwiches, and mac and cheese.

Wanting my partner Nancy to know places I loved growing up, we have driven around Tahoe. We also considered purchasing a Summer place on Prince Edward Island, where we vacationed

Life Abundant

early during our Canadian years. At the time, our sons complained that these locations were too distant from southern Ontario where we lived from 1976–1975 and since 2008.

In the eighties and early nineties, Hamilton neighbours and a McMaster University colleague often spoke of cottaging at Pointe au Baril, a town some two hundred miles (or three hundred thirty kilometers) north of Hamilton on the Georgian Bay of Lake Huron. Located at the end of what was once accessible only by rail or boat, Pointe au Baril took its name from a historic lighthouse, part of a system that includes buoys and markers to guide boaters through the shoals that cover the eastern coast of Georgian Bay. The area features spectacular forests, rocky cliffs, and some thirty thousand islands. While farmland once dotted the mainland, the area has more recently been primarily a place of recreation and source of income for permanent residents.

One weekend in October 1992, when some cottages become available for sale at the end of the season, Nancy and I met a real estate agent who later became our nearest neighbour. He took us to a number of cottages in the rain. Despite less than perfect conditions, we were smitten by the beauty of the area. To our amazement, we were able to purchase an unpretentious cottage within our budget and a modest motorboat needed to get to and from our island.

Unexpectedly, only two years after our purchase, we moved to Memphis, Tennessee. Our cottage became the magnet drawing us back to Ontario every Summer. Subsequently, for over thirty years, *Mimissing Keewadin* (island of the north wind) has provided seasonal recreation, respite, and release from pressures of contemporary living.

When asked what we do there, I like to say "nothing." When pressed, I add that we fish, canoe, kayak, swim, read, feast, nap on a hammock, take photographs, and explore nearby waters, woodlands, and wild areas. We supplement our food stock by picking wild blackberries, blueberries, strawberries, or cranberries or by catching perch, small-mouth bass, or walleye (also known as yellow pickerel).

Two Lakes

Early in our Pointe au Baril years, we purchased a small Laser sailboat. I had previously tried my hand at sailing when vacationing on Prince Edward Island in Eastern Canada. Nancy and I visited a former student, Joe Gehiere, who encouraged me to join him in a small sailboat. I did, but unexpected winds came up. Seeing that Joe and I were being taken out to sea—specifically the Atlantic Ocean—Joe's wife, Donna, called upon the Coast Guard to rescue us.

Despite this experience, I tried again at Pointe au Baril, especially since my sons were more skilled boatsmen. After nearly grounding myself on a couple occasions, I concluded the sport was not for me. I can only enjoy watching neighboring cottagers who sail in our area.

Nancy and I sometimes cross our island on foot or by canoe on a small lake behind our cottage. As well, we are a short boat ride from a public dock on Friend Island. After a short hike, we watch magnificent sunsets. For longer hikes, we visit two nearby provincial parks. After a twenty-minute boat ride to the mainland, Killbear is about forty kilometres to the south. Grundy is about an hour to the north. There we swim on sandy beaches, hike and enjoy picnics. On such outings, we do our best to avoid rocks that could damage a boat motor prop, and other hazards such as poison ivy and various critters: blackflies, mosquitos, black bears, and eastern massasauga rattlers, an endangered species and the only venomous snake in Ontario.

Several years ago, son Matthew's future Ph.D. advisor at the University of Arkansas, Fayetteville, hosted a welcome party for new students. Matt noticed a photograph of a massasauga on one of the walls of his professor's home. When Matt identified the rattler to his professor, an inland water fish specialist, Matt learned his supervisor had also studied them.

Massasaugas are not, of course, to be played with. Though a bite is not likely to be fatal, I prefer not to require an emergency visit to the nursing station in town, or the hospital at Parry Sound. We take precautions such as sprinkling salt around the area of our cottage.

A prominent feature near us is Hole-in-the-wall, a narrow passage often mentioned in guide-books to the area. Going through it is a boating nightmare, what with swimmers and kids jumping from the cliffs and other boats. One can stop at a beach where, mid- to late June, there are few crowds and the water is finally around twenty degrees Celsius, or in September after Labour Day when most cottagers have returned home.

Over the years, we have averaged six or seven weeks at the cottage each Summer. In addition, both sons have enjoyed weeks alone with their families. As well, our older grand-daughters Abbey and Emma have generally spent a few days with us.

As I write, climate change which is impacting our area. Forest fires are more numerous. Invasive plant and animal species are wrecking havoc. The Georgian Bay Biosphere Reserve that stretches some two hundred kilometers along the eastern Georgian Bay is one local response. One of nineteen such sites in Canada, members of the local Pointe au Baril Islanders' Association work to protect hundreds of endangered species of plants, animals and insects.

Nancy and I are grateful to join, however modestly, in protecting the Georgian Bay. Committed to stewardship of our endangered planet, we identify with the Seventh Generation Principle of the Iroquois people. Decisions we make today about the energy, water, and other natural resources that we use contribute to a sustainable world seven generations into the future. This puts the onus on us to ensure our lifestyle contributes not simply to our enjoyment of our good earth, but also to its abundance for future generations.

30

Community Activities

I HAVE BEEN ACTIVE in various community organizations. Though I never met him in person, one individual in particular influenced my activism. Over the years, I had read several books by the Reverend Dr. Martin Luther King, Jr. In 1986, I attended events in Atlanta marking the first US Martin Luther King, Jr. Holiday. I signed and have ever since carried a card with a Living the Dream pledge "to do everything that I can to make America and the world a place where equality and justice, freedom and peace will grow and flourish. I commit myself to living the dream by loving, not hating; showing understanding, not anger; making peace, not war."

Drawing on this covenant, I co-chaired with a close friend, Joy Warner, a coalition of Hamilton-area peace and justice groups through the 1980s and early 1990s. At an annual Mother's Day walk for peace, we recalled the appeal of nineteenth-century activist Julia Ward Howe who, in 1870, wrote to "womanhood throughout the world" as follow,

> Arise, then, women of this day! Arise all women who have hearts, whether our baptism be that of water or of tears! . . . We women of one country will be too tender of those of another country to allow our sons to be trained to injure theirs. From the bosom of the devastated earth

a voice goes up with our own. It says "Disarm, Disarm! The sword of murder is not the balance of justice.¹

Hamilton's Mother's Day Walk for Peace celebrated our potential to create and sustain more peaceful communities where all people are valued and have what they need. Aware of a need for a spiritual foundation of such activism, several of us began to meet once weekly at seven in the morning for an hour of prayer. We did not discuss wider issues, nor did we plan other events. We sometimes shared a pot-luck at our home, or that of other members.

At the time of writing, I am active in varying degrees with several organizations. One, Amnesty International, is a human rights organization supported by millions of people in over a hundred and seventy countries and territories. During the 1980s, I served as chair of a local group and on the national board, with specific responsibility for a campaign protesting abuses in Uganda. Nancy hosted another group that met in our home. While modest, such efforts—combined with those of others—promote care of earth, democracy, human rights, and peace. Do they have any impact?

In some measure, yes. Let me provide three examples. One concerns my participation over many years in a worldwide campaign challenging Apartheid in South Africa. On September 12, 1985 I participated in an act of civil disobedience at the Toronto offices of Bata shoes. Protesting the company's use of labour in one of the so-called South African homelands, eight of us were arrested, charged with blocking and defacing access to the headquarters with our blood. We were quickly released, likely because the company did not want a case to go to trial. I realized then, that by putting myself on the line, I was not powerless to act in the face of evil.²

At the time I served on the Academic Senate of McMaster University. I introduced a motion calling on the university board to divest of investments in South Africa. When the motion passed, Ken Post, a personal friend as well as assistant to McMaster's

---

1. https://tile.loc.gov/storage-services/service/rbc/rbpe/rbpe07/rbpe074/07400300/07400300.pdf.

2. For an account, see my "There Is a Time to Resist," *Canadian Baptist* 132, 3 (March 1986) 7–9.

COMMUNITY ACTIVITIES

president, Alvin Lee, cautioned that it would be difficult to develop an investment policy free of any challenge on ethical grounds. In response, I argued that by its action, McMaster contributed to growing international pressure that would ultimately culminate in majority rule in South Africa.

We believed that, by our action, publicity generated exposed how Canada's political system protected the property rights of a company that profited from business operations involving human suffering elsewhere. Also, we were encouraged that our action sparked similar efforts at other universities around Canada.

By the early 1990s, with cascade-like momentum, universities worldwide divested from companies doing business in South Africa. Such efforts ultimately culminated in South Africa's transition to majority rule. One step in this direction took place in February 1990 when, in his speech at the opening of Parliament, President de Klerk announced the repeal of the ban on the African National Congress and the release of political prisoners from jail. On February 11, a leading activist, Nelson Mandela was released after twenty-seven years in prison. Three years later, on May 10, 1994, Nelson Mandela was inaugurated as the first black president of South Africa. With others I watched his inauguration on television.

As a second example, I have been deeply committed to the struggle for international peace. In the 1980s, I worked with McMaster University colleagues to develop a peace studies program. As a start, I co-taught an introductory course with the late Graeme MacQueen, a colleague in the Religious Studies Department, and Joanna Santa Barbara, a physician and member of McMaster's Health Science faculty. Among achievements in the 1980s, we established an annual lectureship, the Bertrand Russell Peace Lectures and organized several conferences. One of them, "Nonviolent Initiatives for Social Change in Central America and the Middle East," was held from June 16—30, 1989 for which Graeme MacQueen edited and published the papers in *Unarmed Forces: Nonviolent Action in Central America and the Middle East* (Toronto: Canadian Papers in Peace Studies, 1992). Subsequently, hundreds of students have taken courses in the program, and some have gone on to work in peace and justice organizations.

Another group with which I have been involved for over a decade is Democracy Probe International (DPI), an independent nonpartisan organization of physical and life scientists, engineers, humanists, social scientists, lawyers, teachers, writers, and activists. Based in Canada but with an international purview, DPI members seek ways to replace the corrupting influence of corporate rule with an authentic democracy in the way we are governed as well as in the way we live and work in our communities. We believe that authentic democracy offers, among its many benefits, the best hope of stifling war and halting the accelerating pace of environmental destruction that poses an existential threat to civilization. DPI members promote initiatives for the restoration and development of democratic practices and institutions.

We began meeting in 2014 and organized public gatherings. These became impossible in 2020 after the Covid-19 pandemic spread from China to North America. Since then, a few of us have continued to meet weekly by Zoom. In the future we may resume public gatherings. As well, some of us, myself included regularly write op-ed pieces or letters to the editor published in *The Hamilton Spectator* and elsewhere.

Another organization with which I have identified is the Gandhi Peace Festival, which started in Hamilton in 1993 as a way to celebrate the hundred and twenty-fifth anniversary of the birth of Gandhi (1869–1948) and, more generally, India's rich cultural history. Subsequently, every year, the Festival has chosen a theme and speaker who addresses the theme in a lecture on campus, and at the Hamilton City Hall or Peace Garden for a wider audience. The events generally occur on the weekend closest to Gandhi's birthday (October 2). Support by a diverse group of organizations and individuals and the work of numerous volunteers have made the Festival a vibrant event.

In connection with the peace festival, the Indian community gifted the city of Hamilton with a statue of Gandhi that was installed in the gardens in front of city hall. Nancy recalls accompanying a class of our granddaughter Emma on a field trip downtown. As they passed the Gandhi statue, one of the students asked who this was. Emma responded, "That's Gandhi. My grandfather teaches about him."

During the 1980s, I taught a course on Gandhi, King, Tolstoy and Nonviolence at McMaster University. As well, I served on the Human Rights commission of the Baptist World Alliance. Meeting in Melbourne, Australia in January 2000, I led a workshop on the Reverend Dr. Martin Luther King, Jr. and Gandhi after which I traveled to India where I invited to teach at a Baptist seminary in Nagaland. Due to unrest in that part of the country, I was barred from traveling widely. My hosts reorganized the setting. I delivered the course in India's capital, New Delhi. Gandhi and Dr. King have thus inspired and mentored my life abundant.

31

Gandhian *Swadeshi* in Colombia

FOR TWO WEEKS IN August 2009, I was part of a human rights delegation to Colombia organized by FOR's Bogotá office. Upon arrival, we learned about the Colombia context from national leaders and international agencies such as the United Nations High Commission for Human Rights and the United Nations High Commission for Refugees, representatives of which estimate over four million or about ten percent of the country's population was internally displaced. We also explored issues under discussion in North America including free trade agreements and proposals related to locating US bases in the Global South.

We continued to San José de Apartadó, a village collective near the Gulf of Urabá in northwest Colombia. In the 1960s and 1970s, farmers participated in cooperative agriculture. As the country descended into civil war, the community suffered two massacres. In response, several hundred persons declared themselves a Peace Community. With the support of the region's Catholic Bishop, San José Peace Community members pledged to remain neutral amidst escalating violence and extrajudicial killings. Demanding their right to justice and peace, they committed to the following:

1. To farm in cooperative work groups
2. To denounce the injustice and impunity of armed actors committing extrajudicial killings
3. Not to bear arms
4. Not to participate in armed conflict in direct or indirect forms
5. Not to manipulate or give information to any party involved in armed conflict.

Around the time of our visit, Community members experienced political violence, mostly at the hands of paramilitary groups supported by the Colombian Army. On February 21, 2005, the army killed the Peace Community's founder and seven others. Afterwards, the presence of both military and paramilitary in the area grew. As a result, international peace and justice groups such as FOR, Peace Brigades International, and Witness for Peace joined small Colombian human rights groups in seeking to protect indigenous communities when threats or attacks occur.

As well, due in part to international lobbying, in early 2005, more than US $70 million of military aid for Colombia was put on hold. While the aid was eventually released days before Colombia's president met with then President George W. Bush, this delay reflected growing concern by the Department of State and human rights groups regarding cases reportedly involving direct violations by the Colombian Army.

Such efforts led the Colombian government to give the appearance of taking steps to protect the lives and personal integrity of the Peace Community members. In a meeting with representatives of state security forces, delegation members received a booklet that explained efforts by the military to protect community members. We were asked to encourage victims to come forward for help.

Peace community members are suspicious of such overtures. They honour their basic commitments not to cede to the threat of death, nor to collaborate with any party in any way. As one person put it, "The truth is a beacon that guides us, enabling us to maintain our principles and hope that someday all these actors of terror will be brought to justice." A victims' rights representative informed our delegation that there have been over sixty thousand state crimes registered since the 1960s and that the number of unregistered must be much higher. This included murder of an estimated twenty-five hundred labour union organizers. A lawyer told us that denouncing crimes of the state carries a weightier jail sentence (six to ten years) than actually committing such crimes (five to eight years). Colombian intelligence forces conduct surveillance of anyone vaguely working around issues of peace or human rights, including the FOR offices.

Acts of terror against peace community members have continued. In 2009 alone sixty-seven indigenous persons were murdered; none of their killers were arrested. On June 13, around 8 a.m., members of the army destroyed the cocoa bean garden of two Peace Community members in the village of La Union. They told another inhabitant that the community is a guerrilla community and that sooner or later they would be exterminated. On June 19th and 20th, a group of about one hundred armed paramilitaries travelled through the villages of Rodozali, La Hoz, Mulatos and La Esperanza dressed in khaki with insignia of the AUC [the acronym for a notorious paramilitary group known in English as United Self Defence Forces of Colombia].

Sixteen years later, I continue to receive reports of violence against Peace Community. Members continue to be largely self sufficient, and to market organically farmed products (coffee, chocolate, small bananas, and plantain) through fair trade companies. In such a way, the community illustrates the principle of *swadeshi*, a Hindi word for local self-improvement. The term derived from Gandhi's successful economic strategy to boycott foreign goods and encourage the domestic production.

In 2004, Peace Community members organized a minga, a form of Andean indigenous collective analysis and decision making. People respond non-violently to oppression while respecting the humanity of their opponents. One person explained the communities actions, "We can not remain victims. We will be free through our collective action."

In learning of the minga, a phrase *ser para tener o tener para ser* spoke to the delegation; namely: Are we born to possess or do we seek what we need in order to live? This recalled for me a passage in Deuteronomy 30, cited often in the anti-nuclear demonstrations of the 1980s, where Yahweh, offering a way of life or a way of death, calls upon people to choose the way of life. Perhaps those presently governing Colombia and the rich North, representing the powerful economic elites of the world, will come to see that theirs is a way of death. Earth can not bear the greed of the few.

It is amazing how committed Peace Community members and activists are. They carry on despite their circumstances, aware that many of them may not witness change in their own lifetime. What can we do in North America to help counter impunity and guarantee the rights of all Colombian citizens? Those we met emphasized that our presence helps them to show the government that the world is watching. They also mentioned the need for mobilization. International citizens must continue to press the Colombian government to abide by international humanitarian law and share victims' stories to a wider audience. For their part, Colombian activists draw strength in numbers. As a representative concluded, "Mobilizations bring people from darkness into light."

In 2016, Colombian President Juan Manuel Santos received the Nobel Peace Prize for his efforts to end decades of conflict during which an estimated two hundred and sixty thousand people died, and more than six million internally displaced. While I am not so naive to believe that our delegation contributed to the peace accord for which President Santos was honored and which was narrowly rejected in a referendum, I do understand that our support for the courageous work of grassroots communities in Colombia strengthened their capacity to wage peace despite the murder of many community members. Believing, in words of the World Social Forum, that another world is possible, the Peace Community of San José de Apartadó inspired me, and others to join in building a new Colombia, and a better world for all.

For nearly fifteen years since my visit, FOR has maintained a permanent presence in La Unión. Volunteers live in the community and walk with village members from one community to another. Peace Presence Colombia continues to urge the wider world to support the community by buying fair trade products such as coffee and cocoa and to protest human rights violations. For current information about the community, see https://peacepresence.org/about-us/. Through prayerful support of the ability of Columbians to live in safety, I seek not only to ensure that community members continue to thrive and that their witness to possibilities of living more abundantly becomes better known around the world.

32

Tomato Soup and Grilled Cheese Sandwiches

EARLY IN OUR HAMILTON years, I discovered a radio program called the Royal Canadian Air Farce. Each Sunday at 1:00 p.m., it featured political and cultural satire. Broadcast from 1973 to 1997, it subsequently moved to television until December 2008.

To listen, I hastened home from worship and prepared a simple lunch of tomato soup and grilled cheese sandwiches. In advance, Nancy often made home-made tomato soup. Otherwise, I opened a Campbell's can, or when away, whatever alternative was available. Until I adopted a pescatarian diet, I often added a slice of ham.

While the Canadian Air Farce gave way to other programming, I continue to prepare tomato soup and grilled cheese sandwiches virtually every Sunday afternoon. Why? Tradition. Composer Jerry Bock and lyricist Sheldon Harnick included a piece entitled "Tradition" in the Broadway hit *Fiddler on the Roof*. The song captures the power of traditions. Some change. Some remain the same.

When they visit at home or at the cottage, our sons, grandchildren and even friends have come to expect a grilled cheese sandwich and tomato soup for lunch. I rarely fail. Accordingly, tomato soup and grilled cheese sandwiches have become very much a part of my abundant life.

33

Reflections on Turning Eighty

TURNING EIGHTY HAS COME as a shock. I am an old man. Before too long, my life abundant will give way to another that I can only consider as mystery. From family, friends, communities in which I have chosen to live and companions with whom I have worked and, sometimes, organized for positive social change, I have learned to live in the now, to remain open to the new, to expect the unanticipated and to be grateful for what truly has been a life abundant.

Readers who—like Nancy and myself—have written many letters of protest through Amnesty International or other organizations may wonder if anything that you have done has made a difference. Perhaps not in every instance. However, once in a while I have received confirmation that such advocacy matters.

In 1994, for example, I received a note from Christiaan Frederick Beyers Naude (1915-2004), Afrikaner theologian and leading anti-apartheid activist before South Africa's first non-racial elections. For years I had sent him a post card (easier for security guards to read) greeting him at Christmas. In his letter, Beyers Naude thanked me for my annual card and expressed thanks for sustaining his hope for a positive outcome in the anti-apartheid struggle.

Similarly, in 1992, as director of McMaster's peace studies program, I invited Elena Bonner (1923-2011), wife of Nobel

Peace Prize winner Andrei Sakharov, to deliver the Bertrand Russell Peace Lectures at McMaster. She came and gave three lectures on the theme "Human Rights and National Self-Determination in the Former Soviet Union." Understanding she rarely accepted such invitations, I asked why had she accepted. She took a letter out of her purse and said, "I know who you are and what you have contributed to our struggle for freedom." The letter was a copy of one that I and written of my protests against Sakharov's incarceration.

Many former students have commented to me about the value not only of the content of what I taught, but also—or perhaps most especially—of an assignment, regularly to do some community service. Modeling what I asked of students, I have for years done such community service.

In 1981, I wrote two articles growing out of my reading *Limits to Growth* and *Mankind at the Turning Point* by the Club of Rome. I cited an old French riddle that described the predicament faced by humanity:

> Let's suppose you own a lake about a quarter of a mile across. Near the shore a variety of water lily is growing that has an unusual characteristic—it doubles in size every day. If the lily pads grow unchecked it will cover the pond in thirty days, blocking out all light and oxygen, blocking off other forms of life in the lake. For weeks, the lily seems small and you are busy, so you ignore it and go about your own business, deciding to deal with it when it covers close to half the pond. On what day will that be? On the 29th day, of course. You have one day left to save the pond.[1]

We are now on day twenty-nine. To counteract accelerating climate catastrophe, humanity must act with urgency akin to the Marshall Plan, by which the US aided Europe to recover from World War II. We must replace consumerism, consumption and capitalism with conservation, communalism and conversion by which I mean changing to renewable energy sources and work

---

1. "The Party Goes On. God's People in the Age of Scarcity," *Canadian Baptist* 127 (February 1981) 11.

with local communities to find ways to live more simply than the life style enjoyed by my generation of North American elites.

In North America, the dominant socioeconomic and cultural system encourages us to define our success, our very happiness, through how much we consume, how much we travel, how rich our diet, how big our house, how fancy our car, and on and on. However seductive this life style is and however brilliantly we—Canadians and US Americans—export the model, the current population of the world population, 8,213,269,530 as of Friday, March 28, 2025 per recent United Nations estimates, cannot sustain such abuse of our rose, our finite planet.[2]

Many people now grasp how fatally flawed the current economic system in North America is. It contributes, or enables the rich to profit, while at the same time we are shortening life expectancy, increasing stress and social isolation as well as wrecking havoc on global and local environments. We must seek to relate to the earth in new ways in the hope that, as more and more people make such a move, a new ecological ethic will emerge to help all humanity to live more abundantly.

---

2. https://www.worldometers.info/world-population/.

34

Dream of God and Concluding Reflections

> The Lord spoke to Moses on Mount Sinai, saying . . . when you enter the land that I am giving you, the land shall observe a Sabbath for the Lord. Six years you shall sow your field, and six years you shall prune your vineyard, and gather in their yield; but in the seventh year there shall be a Sabbath of complete rest for the land, a Sabbath for the Lord: you shall not sow your field or prune your vineyard. You shall not reap the aftergrowth of your harvest or gather the grapes of your unpruned vine: it shall be a year of complete rest for the land. You may eat what the land yields during its Sabbath . . . [and] on the Day of Atonement—you shall have the trumpet sounded throughout all your land. And you shall hallow the fiftieth year and you shall proclaim liberty throughout the land to all its inhabitants. It shall be a Jubilee for you it shall be holy. (Leviticus 25:1–12)

IN THE CREATION ACCOUNTS in Genesis, God placed the first humans in Eden, a garden that individuals could tend and where they could enjoy the fruits of their labor. However, because of their disobedience, God drove these humans from Eden. This symbolized the broken relationship between God and humans. Thereafter,

Dream of God and Concluding Reflections

much of the *Bible* describes God's will that humans live in harmony with the Holy One and with each other.

To describe Eden restored, biblical writers used diverse images like peaceable kingdom (Isaiah 11:1–9), new creation (2 Corinthians 5:17), new heaven and earth (Isaiah 65:17–19), and Jubilee (Leviticus 25:1–12). In 2000, organizers of the Jubilee Movement sought debt relief for poor nations.

As I conclude this book, I underscore an image, *Dream of God*, title of a book by Verna J. Dozier. A secondary school teacher and Episcopal religious educator, Dozier characterized the dream of God as reconciling rebellious humans to the Creator and creation. Nancy and I first read her book as part of a servant leadership group in Memphis, Tennessee. As we reflected on Dozier's book, we sought to incorporate her ideas in our journeys inward (prayer and meditation) and outward (worship and using our gifts in community service).

Ancient prophets like Isaiah and Saint Paul and modern ones like Verna Dozier challenge humans to be midwives of the dream of God. Indeed, this is how I see my role in writing this book. Not experienced as a medical midwife, I sincerely pray that my words may encourage readers to share in birthing the dream of God.

Adapting words of the Leviticus text, the contemporary songwriter Mary Chapin Carpenter sang of Jubilee on her album *Stones on the Rock*. Her question resonates, can you imagine you are like a frail boat on a vast sea scanning the night for a great guiding light that announces the day of Jubilee?[1]

Over the years, I have made many key decisions, including especially my asking Nancy to marry. Another was to resign from the US Department of State without a certain professional future. Yet another was the decision to retire relatively early from full time employment and return to the Hamilton area. This permitted Nancy and me to have a wonderful relationship with two of our grandchildren. Over many years, we picked Abbey and Emma up after school, watched them at sports and shared cottage time and other happy moments of their lives. Living in Ontario, we regret

1. https://www.youtube.com/watch?v=X8TRSLLgmMs.

LIFE ABUNDANT

that this has not been possible for our other two grandchildren Drake and Nadine who at time of writing live in California.

Prayerfully, I have written these stories both to reflect on my life of abundance, and to encourage readers to pause and discern ways to reflect on the greater common good. The Dutch painter Vincent van Gogh (1853–1890) once articulated this vision:

> Many people would undoubtedly think it foolish and superstitious to believe still in a change for the better. Sometimes, it is in winter so bitingly cold that one says, "It is too cold, what do I care if there is a summer to follow? The evil surpasses by far the good." But with or without our permission there comes an end last to the bitter frost, and on a certain morning the wind has turned and we have a thaw. Comparing the state of the weather to our state of mind and our circumstances—like the weather subject to changes and variety—I have still some hope left for a change for the better.[2]

At the outset of this book, I acknowledged that I was writing at a challenging time. I do not believe that it is the will of the Holy One that the world should continue as currently is the case, riven by war, human rights violations, and ecological catastrophe. Such is not consistent with the world I dream. Like Van Gogh, and the World Social Forum, of which I attended sessions in Caracas, Venezuela and Detroit, Michigan, I am inspired by the movement's theme that another world is possible. A poster with these words on my desk daily remind me that another world is possible.[3]

Since 2001, the World Social Forum has brought together non-governmental organizations, advocacy campaigns, and myriad social movements to promote international solidarity and concrete action towards a more democratic and more just world and to build alternatives to neoliberalism. The second gathering that I attended, in Detroit, Michigan in 2009, coincided with recognition

2. *Pax Christi*, 54.

3 https://upsidedownworld.org/archives/venezuela/the-world-social-forum-and-the-street-in-caracas-venezuela/. https://www.academia.edu/1029 39176/World_Social_Forum_2009_Time_to_Bring_the_WSF_to_the_USA.

of the Martin Luther King Jr. national holiday in the US. I found it stirring to witness the scope of organizing for social change represented by the organizations and individual participants. I was living a concrete embodiment of King's legacy in the decades that have followed since his murder in Memphis in 1968.

While Dr. King was not the only dreamer, he worked actively, successfully, and in some senser subversively for change. Similarly, those in contemporary movements for change advocate and work to promote the greater common good. One objective for writing this book has been to invite others to get involved in such efforts by rooting out some of the human causation of climate change and related environmental and socio-economic problems.

To this end, I have identified with local Hamilton activists to promote the United Nations Declaration on a Culture of Peace and Non-Violence. Working on the basis of a set of principles with the goal of preventing violence and violent conflicts, community activists have offered workshops and other events promoting an alternative to the culture of war through education for peace, the promotion of sustainable economic and social development, respect for human rights, equality between women and men, democratic participation, tolerance, the free flow of information, and disarmament.

Throughout my teaching career, I have encouraged others to explore and develop knowledge, values, and skills needed to realize a more sustainable way of life than that we have inherited. I have often cited the parable of the mustard seed, a well-known teaching of Jesus recorded in Mark 4:30–32 (parallel texts are Matthew 13:31–32 and Luke 13:18–19). Jesus uses this imagery to illustrate the nature and growth of the realm of God. The story emphasizes the possibility of transformation growing from simple beginnings.

Similarly, I have often emphasized the need not to measure success by results. Since the early 1960s, when I began reading essays and books by the monk Thomas Merton, I have been mindful of Merton's advice to a young peace activist, Jim Forest, in a February 21, 1966 letter:

> Do not depend on the hope of results. When you are doing the sort of work you have taken on, essentially an apostolic

work, you may have to face the fact that your work will be apparently worthless and even achieve no result at all, if not perhaps results opposite to what you expect.... As for the big results, these are not in your hands or mine, but they can suddenly happen, and we can share in them, but there is no point in building our lives on this personal satisfaction, which may be denied us and which after all is not all that important.... The great thing after all is to live, not to pour out your life in the service of a myth: and we turn the best things into myths. If you can get free from the domination of causes and just serve Christ's truth, you will be able to do more and will be less crushed by the inevitable disappointments.... The real hope, then, is not in something we think we can do, but in God who is making something good out of it in some way we cannot see. If we can do His will, we will be helping in this process. But we will not necessarily know all about it beforehand.[4]

And so, as I navigate my eighties, I am hopeful. I am not alone but live in God's world. The Holy One who has guided me through eighty years plus continues to work in me and others by the Spirit.[5] Filled with gratitude and dreams, I have been privileged to live a life of abundance, breadth of opportunity, depth of friendships, and emotional, intellectual, and spiritual growth. In the Broadway musical, *Les Misérables*, the cast sings of a world they dream. With them I ask, "Is there a world you long to see?" Longing to see a different world, I hear distant drums that portend the future about which they bring, "when tomorrow comes."

I long to see a world in which all people live in right relationship with the Holy One, however named or understood. Sharing life together with one another and with creation, I have been blessed to live abundantly. While humankind has a long, long way before we realize the Beloved Community of which the Reverend Dr. King spoke, I give thanks to the Holy One for the gift of abundance in my life and in the lives of many others.

---

4. Thomas Merton to James Forest, *Essential Writings*, 135–36.

5. https://united-church.ca/community-and-faith/welcome-united-church-canada/faith-statements/new-creed-1968.

Appendix 1

Las Lomas graduation address, 1961, Ever the Faith Endures

MAN NEVER IS; HE is becoming. Life is a process of change, for nothing remains static. Life is a continuous search for those ideals, those causes, those convictions to which we must give ourselves, wholly, uncompromisingly, for greatness is not equated to inertness or to indecision. We must move always toward the future, for the future becomes the now, and the now is the appointed time. As we are certain of the present, so must we be assured of the future.

A poet once expressed these thoughts:

> Nothing that lives stands still.
> Grow it must, or shrink.
> There is no alternative.
> Only inanimate things are static, fixed.
> Marble remains unchanged;
> The living creature changes always:
> Expands, increases—or retrogrades, withers to decay.

Must we be lifeless, without distinction? NO! Life is more than existence; life is change—change in political life, social life, economic life, and personal life. Reality changes swiftly and often violently. Each moment has infinite potential. We, as individuals, must not recede from the dynamic to the passive. We cannot be

Appendix 1

passive, for restlessness is discontent, and discontent is the greatest necessity for progress. We must struggle toward those ideals and for those causes which we believe in, but always with firm, persevering conviction, not by stressing "sometimes" or "perhaps." Let us remember the following:

> Socrates—poisoned for those ideals which are taught yet today.
>
> Saint Paul—persecuted for an unwavering faith.
>
> Marin Luther—excommunicated for expressing great concepts of reform.
>
> Charles Darwin—hated for teaching evolution, a conviction that he believed resolutely.

These were men of individuality and greatness who defended their beliefs with complete faith against suffocating opposition. In order not to compromise our destinies, we too must have faith—faith in our causes, ourselves, and an eternal Preserver, infinite and omnipotent. We walk not by sight, which dwells in the present, but by faith, which creates our tomorrows.

In "Ode to the West Wind," the poet Percy Bysshe Shelley asks, "If Winter comes, can Spring be far behind?"[1] Greatness can be achieved, but we must have determined faith that tomorrow will inspire us to the fulfillment of our goals. Ever the faith has endured. Now the world senses improvements envisioned by other men of greatness and of faith. Men once mocked electricity and the airplane. Some thought the world was flat. Today we have atomic energy applicable to peace and jet airplanes encircle the globe. Tomorrow men will trap solar energy and stream to celestial bodies; colonizing the moon will be insufficient for a galactic team. The future will come for us also. "The sundown is tomorrow's wisdom; today is going to be a long, long ago."

---

1. https://www.poetryfoundation.org/poems/45134/ode-to-the-west-wind.

Appendix 2

Application for Conscientious Objector Status, June 1, 1967

I BELIEVE IN GOD, who creates, sustains, infuses with, and indwells our lives. God is love; God is justice; God is Truth; God is absolute. Yet these descriptive qualities by which I as a finite being seek to explain my belief in a Supreme Being are unable fully to describe the nature of God. God is not to be contained by any definition, schema, theology, or plan. All humans can do is to grasp at parts of the Divine's total being and mystery. For God is solely and singularly free, the absolute resolution of all paradox and contradiction.

God has expressed the God-self through creation; to the prophets; in the person of a Son; and by the Holy Spirit. God has revealed the fulness of human beingness in Christ Jesus, my Lord and Savior, the ground of my life's commitment, being, and confidence, the motivating force of my ministry in discipleship. Through divine power and spirit, God strengthens and guides me. God is my primary locus and framework of authority in life, the ground of my conscience by which I necessarily determine ethical decisions. God's call to discipleship—to turn from self to others—is a call to live in accord with God's will.

Peace—which exegetes the meaning of reconciliation through the New Testament—is a primary concept that explicates my understanding of relationship to God and humanity. In Romans 5 and Ephesians 2, there is a subtle connection between reconciliation and peace, between individual reconciliation of people to God and corporate reconciliation among all people.

Peace is the very gift of reconciliation, which was accomplished on the Cross. For the early convert Paul, "since we are justified by faith, we have peace with God through our Lord Jesus Christ" (Rom. 5:1). In other words, we are right-wised, we have peace with God. In the letter to the Ephesians, peace is so very much a consequence of the cross that Christ is understood as the very peace we have gained and have. Peace assumes an ongoing and consequently eschatological vision; it is clear that we have, today, neither universal social harmony, nor perfect inner peace. But peace is an ongoing and continuing condition which impinges upon our call to discipleship, unto a Lord who shows us the possibility of peace between all people.

We may summarize Biblical ethical thought in several concepts: a proclamation of life; correspondence of ends and means—of which consistency of ethical action and belief is an important corollary; living in the context of the fruits of the Spirit (Galatians 5:22) including love—which includes non-resistance and love for the enemy. These affirmations must apply to social and national relationships, and there is no real scriptural evidence to the contrary. I have struggled with the issue of pacifism for some time, and I am aware of the moral dilemmas so such a position in our times.

In my reading of Union Theological Seminary professor, Reinhold Niebuhr, and others, I recognize that our propensity for sinful action precludes dogmatic perfectionism or absolutism. However, I believe that Jesus set forth the Christian imperative to peacemaking as something morally possible within the compass of human nature, whenever it yields to the living presence of God. I can only hope and pray that all persons of good will realize the need to mobilize human resources to the noble and elevated task which God has designed, beating their swords into plowshares and spears into pruning hoods with the result that the lion and the lamb, the hawk and the dove become one. (Isaiah 2:4 and 11:6–9).

Appendix 3

Ordination Paper, excerpted, May 5, 1971

I OPENED BY CITING Isaiah 21:11–12 (RSV): The oracle concerning Dumah. One is calling to me from Se'ir, "Watchman, what of the night? Watchman, what of the night?" The watchman says: "Morning comes, and also the night. If you will inquire, inquire; come back again and ask." Continuing, I wrote that I cannot imagine a more compelling time to be a Christian, apart from early Christian centuries and the sixteenth century Protestant and Catholic Reformations.

Much that has been meaningful, comforting or unquestioned has been swept away. And in this spring of regeneration, three questions have been raised urgency and clarity: Who is your brother? In response, the civil rights movement notably has lifted up the dignity of all human life. Who is your God? Publication in 1963 of *Honest to God* by Anglican Bishop John A. T. Robinson and the death of God movement have generated debate. And finally, will we survive? The peace movement and critics of technology are vitally concerned with this question.

As Christians wrestled with these questions, a humble peasant from Bergamo, Italy, prayed, "My church and I have shown we can err and falter. It is time to try to do better." To such a prayer from the heart, mind, and soul of Pope John XXIII, the world turned to listen. And the church assumed the posture of powerless and discipleship.

Appendix 3

After my "conversion experience" at the 1958 San Francisco Billy Graham crusade, I joined an American Baptist congregation with a good youth program under the leadership of seminarians. Through this involvement, I first considered the possibility of a professional commitment to ministry.

During my college years, cracks appeared in my faith. I became restless about the God of the four spiritual laws. I became restless about black America, brown America, poor America, violent America, about an America whose false gods were being proclaimed from the pulpits of churches irrespective of denomination. As I read and prayed, I began to reformulate my faith. No second conversion. No flash of light. Rather, the gnawing of faith in a dynamic relationship with a living God whose call is to the razor-thin cutting edges of life. Rather, a cup of cold water. Rather, the process of ministry as a non-violent life-style and a life commitment. These led me to decide to attend seminary.

Initially, my family and some friends did not support this decision. Law school or diplomacy had been my career direction. In the end, they encouraged me and celebrated my offering myself as an empty vessel.

Through my seminary training, I came alive. I thrilled at being able to experience faith and sharpen my understanding of my call. I wrote that there are Biblical passages so difficult and obscure that they are overlooked by almost everyone. This has been the fate of Isaiah 21 with uncertainty as its theme. The idea that I am given a new identity and self-consciousness caught me off guard. Christian identity as that of a watchman. Not a prophet proclaiming ethical norms and moral judgment. Not a warden struggling to preserve the faith of our ancestors. But that of a watchman on aimless night patrol. Uneasy silence. Edgy pacing, back and forth, in the event something breaks.

I wrote of the challenge of sharing one's faith, preaching and teaching at a time when humans had made as mess of things: environmental crisis, racial conflict, urban crisis; crises in foreign relations; limitations and promise of technological innovation; divisions within Christianity and other horrors. It was in such a

Ordination Paper, excerpted, May 5, 1971

world, then, and now, that I responded positively to my call to minister and to share the Gospel of forgiveness and reconciliation. I closed, citing the Cistercian monk Thomas Merton.

> To turn to such a world, in which every other voice but the voice of God is heard and merely to add one more voice to the general din—one's own—is to neglect the ominous reality of a crisis that has become apocalyptic. In "turning to" this kind of world, I think the Catholic Church intends to respect the gravity of its predicament, and to do a little listening. There is certainly an enormous difference between the solemn anathemas of Vatican I and the more temperate and sympathetic appeals of Vatican II for dialogue....
>
> My own peculiar task in my Church and in my world has been that of the solitary explorer who, instead of jumping on all the latest bandwagons at once, is bound to search the existential deaths of faith in its silences, its ambiguities, and in those certainties which lie deeper than the bottom of anxiety. In these depths there are no easy answers, no pat solutions to anything. It is a kind of submarine life in which faith sometimes mysteriously takes on the aspect of doubt when, in fact, one has to doubt and reject conventional and superstitious surrogates that have taken the place of faith. On this level, the division between Believer and Unbeliever ceases to be so crystal clear....
>
> The most hopeful sign of religious renewal is the authentic sincerity and openness with which some Believers are beginning to recognize this. At the very moment when it would seem that they had to gather for a fanatical last-ditch stand, these Believers are dropping their defensiveness, their defiance and their mistrust. They are realizing that a faith that is afraid of other people is no faith at all. A faith that supports itself by condemning others is itself condemned by the Gospel.[1]

With Merton, I share my sense of being a solitary explorer who, instead of jumping on all the latest bandwagons at once, is

---

1. Merton, *Faith and Violence*, 212–14.

Appendix 3

bound to search the existential depths of faith in its silences, ambiguities, and certainties that lie deeper than the bottom of anxiety. In these depths there are no easy answers, no pat solutions to anything. I affirm a kind of submarine life in which faith sometimes mysteriously takes on the aspect of doubt and rejects conventional answers.

Appendix 4

"My Journey in Peacemaking," *Waging Peace in Hamilton*, 2017

AROUND MY TENTH BIRTHDAY, my grandparents Spiridon and Vera Dovjenko gave me a '78 vinyl recording of Peter Ilyich Tchaikovsky's *1812 Overture*. Listening to the real cannon shot and church bells elicited deep emotion. My grandfather wept as he told how his great-grandfather had helped defend our ancestral homeland, Russia against Napoleon.

As a child and teenager, photographs or letters from relatives in distant, mysterious and sometimes alluring places—Australia, Cameroon, China, Israel, and former Yugoslavia—piqued interest in family history. I collected stamps, drew maps, kept photos, and read books like John Reed's *Ten Days that Shook the World* (1919), an eye-witness account of the 1917 Bolshevik revolution led by Lenin that resulted in establishment of the USSR. One commentator cited the film version as characterizing the ambiance at University of California, Berkeley.

Around then, my father served on a jury that found a man guilty of murder and was put to death. My father anguished over his role in what he considered state-murder. Earlier, as a boy growing up in Chita, Siberia, he had witnessed his parents' execution in the Russian Revolution.

Appendix 4

My mother, born in Kiev, Ukraine, lost Jewish family members in the Holocaust. She committed to marrying a non-Jew in part to ensure her children would not so suffer. As able, Mom and Dad brought relatives to North America. Hearing their stories deepened my pacifism.

In high school, I joined Junior Statesmen of America. I debated such issues as the death penalty, just war, and civil defense. Continuing my schooling at the Berkeley campus of the University of California, I was arrested (but not charged) protesting that bomb shelters could not protect us from nuclear annihilation. I attended concerts by Joan Baez, Peter, Paul, and Mary, and others. I protested the growing US buildup in Vietnam. I heard Mario Savio of the Free Speech Movement speak at Sproul Hall on technology in preparation for war:

> . . . and that brings me to the second mode of civil disobedience. There's a time when the operation of the machine becomes so odious, makes you so sick at heart that you can't take part! You can't even passively take part! And you've got to put your bodies upon the gears and upon the wheels, upon the levers, upon all the apparatus—you've got to make it stop! And you've got to indicate to the people who run it, to the people who own it —that unless you're free the machine will be prevented from working at all!!![1]

In the mid-1960s, I signed a Statement of Purpose of the US chapter of the Fellowship of Reconciliation, an international organization that, since World War I, has defended conscientious objectors and provided them opportunities for alternative service. Subsequently, I have served several terms on the National Council of the US branch, chaired a committee that organized its hundredth anniversary, and joined solidarity delegations organized by the US branch to Central America, Vieques, Puerto Rico, where the US tested new weapons systems, and Colombia, where FOR staff and volunteers helped lay seeds for peace culminating in the 2016 Nobel Peace Prize being awarded to the President of Colombia, Juan

---

1. Savio, "Bodies upon the Gears Speech," December 2, 1964.

"My Journey in Peacemaking"

Manuel Santos, for his resolute efforts to bring the country's long civil war to an end, a war that cost the lives of over two hundred thousand Colombians and displaced close to six million people.

During the summer of 1965, I was part of a Crossroads Africa project in Chad. I returned home and did not attend law school, as I had planned. Rather, I enrolled in seminary. Due to its reputation as a liberal hotbed, I chose Colgate Rochester Divinity School in Rochester, New York.

There, *Bible*, ethics, and theology courses deepened my pacifist outlook. I helped form the Flower City Conspiracy through which I protested US involvement in Vietnam. I twice joined marches in Washington, D. C. As well, several of us were arrested blocking entry to a federal court in Rochester. For our defense, we raised money by performing *The Trial of the Catonsville Nine* by Jesuit peace activist Dan Berrigan.

Giving up an automatic draft deferment, I left CRDS at the end of my second year. In applying for conscientious objector status, I summarized my ethics as follows: a) affirmation of life; b) correspondence of ends and means; c) primacy of love of enemy; d) reconciliation; e) living the fruits of the Spirit; and f) non-resistance to evil. I cited the Apostle Paul, ". . .the fruit of the Spirit is love, joy, peace, patience, kindness, generosity, faithfulness, gentleness, and self-control" (Galatians 5:22). I highlighted the assertion of Peter and the apostles, "we must obey God rather than any human authority" (Acts 5:29).

I met with my draft board, which approved my undertaking alternative service as a diplomat with the US Department of State. I served nearly three years in Cameroon and a few months in the Bureau of Educational and Cultural Affairs as special assistant to one of the Deputy Secretaries of State, Alan Anderson Reich. In my last role, I accompanied Kaiser Daliwonga Matanza, chief minister of the Transkei, South Africa, and his wife and assistant, on a month-long American tour.

After I resigned from the US government, I completed my Master of Divinity degree at CRDS followed by studies at the University of Chicago from which I received two degrees, Master of

Appendix 4

Arts (1973) and Doctor of Philosophy (1978). I began teaching in September 1975 at Central Michigan University in Mt. Pleasant, Michigan. I offered introductory courses in religion studies and African religion and history. Despite the promise of tenure, in 1976, I moved to McMaster University in Hamilton, Ontario, Canada where I taught courses in both the university, and McMaster Divinity College.

Once settled in Hamilton, I became involved with McMaster's emerging Centre for Peace Studies. With a friend, Joy Warner, I co-chaired the Hamilton Disarmament Coalition. At our events, I identified as my primary peace community as an ecumenical prayer group that met weekly at the Welcome Inn, a Mennonite ministry in Hamilton's poorer North End. Thursday mornings from seven to eight, we met for an hour of silent meditation and prayer. We shared an occasional meal together and marched together at an annual Mother's Day peace walk.

As well, I helped organize a Canadian Baptist peace group that organized an annual meeting at Ganaraska Woods, a retreat centre part of Calvary Baptist Church in Toronto. We subsequently merged with the BPFNA.

What, from such engagement, do I want to communicate to the next generation? First, "Think Globally, Act Locally." At many peace activities, I have worn a button with this phrase. Through the 1980s and early 1990s, I participated in efforts that led McMaster to twin with a university in El Salvador; to divest of holdings in South Africa; and to create a Centre for Peace Studies. These local initiatives aligned with global efforts to mobilize cultures of peace, a United Nations program aimed at preventing violence and violent conflicts, and to create an alternative to the culture of war and violence.

Second, never doubt that our efforts can make a difference. In 1995, having accepted a position at Memphis Theological Seminary, I met with Willie Herenton, elected in 1991 as Memphis' first African-American mayor. I explained that I was drawn to the city to work towards that time when people would think of Memphis not primarily as where the Reverend Dr. Martin Luther King, Jr., died, but as where Dr. King's vision of the Beloved Community was being realized. To this end, I joined efforts—ultimately successful—to lobby for the City of Memphis and Shelby County to guarantee full-time staff a living wage.

Third, practice gender equality. Co-facilitating HDC with Joy Warner, and co-teaching with female colleagues, I have learned that building a culture of peace requires collegial effort rooted in gender equality. It is no coincidence that creation of the Centre of Peace Studies paralleled the development of Women's Studies as well as Labour Studies and Indigenous Studies at McMaster. Each complemented the other.

Fourth, do not measure success by results. Ever since the early 1960s, when I read Thomas Merton's essay "The Root of War Is Fear" and his anthology *Gandhi on Nonviolence*, I have been mindful of Merton's advice to peace activist Jim Forest not to depend on results.[2]

Fifth, peace work means being peace, as Thich Nhat Hanh, a Buddhist monk formerly active with FOR, has written. Not all peace activists are peaceful. I have tried to face current crises like climate change, war, and the challenge of resettling refugees by joining communities of resistance committed to nonviolence, mindfulness and by efforts to transform violence, fanaticism and dogmatism in myself. Teaching courses about Gandhi, Dr. King, and Thomas Merton as well as regular spiritual retreats, and reading journals like *The Catholic Worker*, *Peace Magazine*, *Ploughshares Monitor*, *Broadview* (successor to the United Church of Canada *Observer*), and *Yes* have nourished my spirituality.

A related practice is Sabbath observance. For years, my e-mail signature highlighted this, "I normally observe Sunday as a Sabbath day when I do not turn on the computer." Words of the Canadian Friends Service Committee summarize how I characterize my journey in peacemaking: "We envision a world in which dignity, justice, peace, human rights, and harmonious relations with creation are fostered and upheld."[3]

2. Merton, *Essential Writings*, 135–36.
3. https://quakerservice.ca/about.

Appendix 4

Finally, I have learned to be persistent, to keep on keeping on. In 1956, during the Montgomery Bus Boycott, an African-American, Mother Poland, observed, "My feets is tired, but my soul is rested." In this spirit, on January 15, 1986, I attended events in Atlanta marking the first US Martin Luther King, Jr. Federal Holiday. I signed and carry in my wallet the "Living the Dream pledge to do everything that I can to make America and the world a place where equality and justice, freedom and peace will grow and flourish. I commit myself to living the dream by loving, not hating; showing understanding, not anger; making peace, not war." My journey in peacemaking continues.

Archival Sources and Bibliography

McMaster University and Canadian Baptist Archives, McMaster Divinity College house papers related to my career. Additional materials are housed at Southern Baptist Historical Library and Archives, 901 Commerce St. #400, Nashville, TN 37203–3630, accessed as the Paul Dekar Collection AR.840.

A Manual of Eastern Orthodox Prayers. London: SPCK, 1945.

Alinsky, Saul D. *Rules for Radicals. A Pragmatic Primer for Realistic Radicals.* New York: Vintage, 1971.

Baldwin, James. *A Fire Next Time.* New York: Vintage, 1963.

Benedict. *The Rule of St. Benedict in English.* Edited by Timothy Fry. Collegeville: Liturgical, 1982.

Berrigan, Daniel. *The Trial of the Catonsville Nine.* Boston: Beacon, 1970.

Bonhoeffer, Dietrich. *Life Together.* Translated from German by John W. Doberstein. New York: Harper & Row, 1954.

Boublil, Alain, and Claude-Michel Schönberg, lyrics by Herbert Kretzmer. *Les Misérables.* 1986.

Buber, *I and Thou.* Translated from German by Walter Kaufmann. New York: Charles Scribner's Sons, 1970.

Burdick, Eugene, and William J. Lederer. *The Ugly American.* New York: Norton, 1958.

Buttry, Daniel, and Damaris Albuquerque. *Healing the World: Gustavo Parajón, Public Health and Peacemaking Pioneer.* Canton: Front Edge, 2023.

Carson, Rachel. *Silent Spring.* New York: Houghton Mifflin, 1962.

Charters, Ann, ed. *The Portable Sixties Reader.* New York: Penguin, 2003.

Chadwick, Owen, ed. *Western Asceticism.* Philadelphia: Westminster, 1958.

Cosby, Gordon. *Handbook for Mission Groups.* Waco: Word, 1975.

Cotter, Jim. *Psalms for a Pilgrim People.* Harrisburg: Morehouse, 1989.

Dekar, Paul R. "A Bird's Eye View of Thich Nhat Hahn." *Fellowship* 83 (Spring 2020) 12–14.

———. *Creating the Beloved Community: A Journey with the Fellowship of Reconciliation.* Scottdale: Herald and Telford: Cascadia, 2005.

Archival Sources and Bibliography

———. "Crossing Religious Frontiers. Christianity and the Transformation of Bulu (Cameroon) Society 1892–1925." PhD thesis, University of Chicago, 1978.

———. *Dangerous People: The Fellowship of Reconciliation Building a Nonviolent World of Justice, Peace, and Freedom*. Virginia Beach: Downing, 2016.

———. *For the Healing of the Nations. Baptist Peacemakers*. Preface by Nancy Sehested. Foreword by Martin E. Marty. Macon: Smyth and Helwys, 1993.

———. "Forging Bonds and Obligations." In *"In an Inescapable Network of Mutuality": Martin Luther King, Jr. and the Globalization of an Ethical Ideal*, co-edited with Lewis V. Baldwin. Foreword by Vicki L. Crawford. Eugene, OR: Cascade, 2013.

———. "From Jewish Mission to Inner City Mission: The Scott Mission and Its Antecedents in Toronto, 1908 to 1964." In *Canadian Protestant and Catholic Missions, 1820s-1960s. Historical Essays in Honour of John Webster Grant*. Edited by John S. Moir and C. T. McIntire. New York: Peter Lang, 1988.

———. *Holy Boldness: Practices of an Evangelistic Lifestyle*. Macon: Smyth and Helwys, 2004.

———. *Journeying with Hope into a New Year. Reflections for Advent and Christmas*. Eugene, OR: Resource Publications, 2011.

———. "Martin Luther King, Jr. and Nonviolent Justice Seekers in Latin America and the Caribbean." In *Nonviolence for the Third Millennium*, edited by G. Simon Harak. Atlanta: Mercer University Press, 2000.

———. "Praying in the Way of Catherine de Hueck Doherty and Thomas Merton." *Merton Seasonal* 48/3 (Fall 2023) 23–26.

———. "The Power of Silence." *Fellowship* 69 (January/February 2003) 15–16.

———. "There Is a Time to Resist." *Canadian Baptist* 132, 3 (March 1986) 7–9.

———. *Thomas Merton: God's Messenger on the Road towards a New World*. Eugene, OR: Cascade, 2021.

———. *Thomas Merton: Twentieth Century Wisdom for Twenty-First Century Living*. Eugene, OR: Cascade, 2011.

Doherty, Catherine de Hueck. *Essential Writings*. Maryknoll, NY: Orbis, 2009.

———. *Poustinia: Christian Spirituality of the East for Western Man*. Notre Dame: Ave Maria, 1974.

Douglas, Mary. *Purity and Danger*. Harmondsworth: Penguin, 1968.

Draper, Hal. *Berkeley: The New Student Revolt*. Introduction by Mario Savio. New York: Grove, 1965.

Forest, Jim. *Living with Wisdom: A Life of Thomas Merton*. Maryknoll, NY: Orbis, 2008.

Francis, Pope. "Address of the Holy Father to a Joint Session of the United States Congress September 24, 2015." *Merton Annual* 28 (2015) 16–23.

Freeman, Jo, and Victoria Johnson. *Waves of Protest: Social Movements since the Sixties*. New York: Rowman & Littlefield, 1999.

Glick, Ted. *Burglar for Peace: Lessons Learned in the Catholic Left's Resistance to the Vietnam War*. Oakland: PM Press, 2020.

Archival Sources and Bibliography

Hamilton, William, and Thomas J. J. Altizer. *Radical Theology and the Death of God*. New York: Bobbs-Merrill, 1966.

Hanh, Thich Nhat. *Being Peace*. Berkeley: Parallax, 1987.

Heath, Gordon L., ed. *Canadian Churches and the First World War*. Eugene, OR: Pickwick, 2014.

Katope, Christopher G., and Paul G. Zolbrod. *Beyond Berkeley: A Sourcebook in Student Values*. Cleveland: World, 1966.

Kaplan, John M. "A Dialogue for Peace between the Jewish and Palestinian Communities in the Memphis Area." *Memphis Theological Seminary Journal* 37 (Fall 2000) 47–59.

Koestler, Arthur. *Darkness at Noon*. Translated from German by Philip Boehm. New York: Scribner, 2019 (1940).

Lipset, Seymour Martin, and Sheldon S. Wolin. *The Berkeley Student Revolt: Facts and Interpretations*. New York: Anchor, 1965.

Marty, Martin E., and R. Scott Appleby. *Fundamentalisms Observed*. Chicago: University of Chicago Press, 1991.

———. *Modern American Religion, Vol. 1: The Irony of It All, 1893–1919*. Chicago: University of Chicago Press, 1986.

———. *Modern American Religion, Vol. 2: The Noise of Conflict 1919–1941*. Chicago: University of Chicago Press, 1991.

———. *Righteous Empire: The Protestant Experience in America*. New York: Dial, 1970.

———. *Varieties of Unbelief*. New York: Holt, Rinehart and Winston, 1964.

Maclean, Norman. *A River Runs Through It*. Chicago: University of Chicago Press, 1977.

McKelvey, Blake. *Rochester. The Quest for Quality 1890–1925*. Cambridge, MA: Harvard University Press, 1956.

Medved, Michael, and David Wallechinsky. *What Really Happened to the Class of '65*. New York: Ballantine, 1976.

Merton, Thomas. *A Search for Solitude: Pursuing the Monk's True Life*. San Francisco: Harper, 1997.

———. *Cold War Letters*. Edited by Christine M. Bochen and William H. Shannon. Maryknoll, NY: Orbis, 2006.

———. *Essential Writings*. Edited by Christine M. Bochen. Maryknoll, NY: Orbis, 2000.

———. *Faith and Violence. Christian Faith and Christian Practice*. Notre Dame: University of Notre Dame Press, 1968.

———, ed. *Gandhi on Non-Violence: A Selection from His Writings*. New York: New Directions, 1963.

———. *Passion for Peace: The Social Essays*. Edited by William H. Shannon. New York: Crossroad, 1995.

Mott, Michael. *The Seven Mountains of Thomas Merton*. London: Sheldon, 1984.

Neufeld, Hugo. *The North End Lives: A Journey through Poverty Terrain*. Waterloo: Herald, 2006.

Archival Sources and Bibliography

Nicholl, Donald. *The Beatitude of Truth. Reflections of a Lifetime.* London: Darton, Longman and Todd, 1997.

———. "Saints for Peace." *Tablet.* January 4, 1992.

Norris, Kathleen. *The Cloister Walk.* New York: Riverhead, 1996.

Pasternack, Boris. *Doctor Zhivago.* Translated from Russian by Max Hayward and Manya Harari. New York: Pantheon, 1958 (1957).

Pearson, Anne M., Khursheed Ahmed, and Joy Warner. *Waging Peace in Hamilton.* Hamilton: Bellwoods, 2017.

O'Connor, Elizabeth. *Journey Inward, Journey Outward.* New York: Harper & Row, 1968.

Rawlyk, G. A. *Is Jesus Your Personal Saviour? In Search of Canadian Evangelicalism in the 1990s.* Kingston: McGill-Queen's University Press, 1996.

Saint-Exupéry, Antoine de. *The Little Prince.* Translated from French by Katherine Woods. New York: Harcourt, Brace & World, 1943.

Savio, Mario. "Bodies upon the Gears Speech." December 2, 1964. https://primevalghosts.com/Savio/Savio.htm.

Sehested, Ken, ed. *Dreaming God's Dream: Study Materials for Church, Home and School.* Charlotte: Baptist Peace Fellowship of North America, 1989.

Sehested, Nancy Hastings. *Marked for Life: A Prison Chaplain's Story.* Maryknoll, NY: Orbis, 2019.

Silberman, Charles E. *Crisis in Black and White.* New York: Random House, 1964.

Sholokhov, Mikhail. *Harvest on the Don.* Translated from Russian by H. C. Stevens. New York: Knopf, 1961 (1935).

Speier, Matthew, ed. *Canadian Peace and World Order Studies: A Curriculum Guide.* Toronto: Association of Canadian Community Colleges, 1987.

Starr, Walter A. Jr. *Guide to the John Muir Trail and the High Sierra Region.* San Francisco: Sierra Club, 1962.

Sutera, Judith, ed. *Work of God: Benedictine Prayer.* Collegeville: Liturgical, 1997.

Wadhwani, R. D. G. "Kodak, FIGHT, and the Definition of Civil Rights in Rochester, New York: 1966–1967." *Historian* 60.1 (Fall 1997) 59–75.

Warshaw, Steven. *The Trouble in Berkeley.* Berkeley: Diablo, 1965.

Weil, Simone. *Waiting on God.* Translated from French by Emma Craufurd. Collins: Fontana, 1950.

www.ingramcontent.com/pod-product-compliance
Lightning Source LLC
Chambersburg PA
CBHW060656100426
42734CB00047B/1962